Cuban Exiles on the Trade Embargo

Cuban Exiles on the Trade Embargo:
Interviews

EDWARD J. GONZÁLEZ

Foreword by Elisabeth C. Aiken

McFarland & Company, Inc., Publishers
Jefferson, North Carolina, and London

LIBRARY OF CONGRESS CATALOGUING-IN-PUBLICATION DATA

González, Edward.
    Cuban exiles on the trade embargo : interviews / Edward J.
González ; foreword by Elisabeth C. Aiken.
        p.   cm.
    Includes index.

    ISBN-13: 978-0-7864-3043-7
    softcover : 50# alkaline paper ∞

    1. Economic sanctions, American — Cuba.   2. United
States — Commerce — Cuba.   3. Cuba — Commerce — United
States.   4. Cuba — Economic conditions — 1990–   5. Cuba —
Social conditions — 1959–   6. Embargo.   I. Title.
    HF1500.5.U5G66   2008
    382'.730973 — dc22   2007021348

British Library cataloguing data are available

Cover photograph ©2007 Blue Moon Stock Photos

Manufactured in the United States of America

*McFarland & Company, Inc., Publishers
    Box 611, Jefferson, North Carolina 28640
    www.mcfarlandpub.com*

In loving memory of my hero
Enrique Anacleto Larrauri
1903–1988

Acknowledgments

Many thanks to Elisabeth C. Aiken, formerly of the English Department at Western Carolina University, currently at Saint Leo University, for her unwavering support and encouragement that enabled me to write this book. Thanks also to Dr. Brian Railsback, current dean of the Honors College at Western Carolina, for his encouragement and for the insights provided during my initial days of this quest.

Thank you to Western Carolina University as a whole, for providing an atmosphere of support to me and all of its students, so we can not only strive to achieve our goals, but are empowered to attain them.

Although there are too many to personally name, I must also must give thanks to the many folks who provided encouragement, or were at least interested in this subject matter and willing to hear me go on and on about it. For these friends, co-workers, and — most importantly — members of my rather large extended family, I am very grateful for your belief in me.

Last but not least, thank you to my wife Theresa for her everlasting patience as I pursued this quest, and my children: Patricia, Emily, Eddy, Sam, Jennifer, and the dynamic duo of Caleb and Conner. I love you.

Ed González
Summer 2007

Contents

Foreword

by ELISABETH C. AIKEN

I first met Ed González during a summer English composition course. Because Ed is a first-generation Cuban American, the research-oriented course became the perfect platform for him to trace his family's Cuban roots and investigate the embargo against Cuba. I considered Ed's unstoppable passion for writing and Cuba an unlooked-for boon that I'd not expected in a routine composition course. His initial assignment was to interview any professional associated with a chosen research topic: in Ed's case, the embargo against Cuba and its effects. Ed quickly e-mailed a questionnaire to several family members, friends, and associates regarding their experiences and beliefs as Cubans and Cuban Americans. The response was extraordinary. Recipients of the email forwarded it to friends, passed it on to extended family, e-mailed Ed with phone numbers of others to contact. He had tapped in to the South Florida community of Cuban Americans eager to share their story, make their voices heard through the filter that is Ed González. With that overwhelming response, this project was born.

Ed's interest in Cuban and Cuban American issues stems not only from his own family's history, but also from his desire to make others, from his small community in western North Carolina, to local Cuban Americans, to exiled heroes in Florida and beyond, aware of the often dire situation just south of our country, of events that led Cuban Americans north from their island — or issues that remain behind them in Cuba. These events need to be addressed by American citizens and our elected leaders. After hearing the voices of Elpidio and Echinque, the forum of La Peña and the beliefs of Father Llorente, we must ask ourselves with candor, *how effective is the embargo against Cuba?*

The opportunity to work with Ed as a fellow writer, and watch him create this series of profiles, has been indescribable. Taking part in the drafting process of this work allowed me to put my classroom ideas and routines to professional — and practical — use. This project gave me the chance to exercise my belief in the written word, in the communication of ideas from writer to reader.

What began as a simple writing assignment has developed into a timely and important piece of writing. I've enjoyed not only learning about the embargo against Cuba, but sharing the excitement of broadcasting different perspectives on that embargo. Cuba is a country with many representative voices, a quality which we, as Americans and citizens of the world, must respect. Taking the time to listen to these stories, to ponder and question the ethics and beliefs behind them, is not a luxury, but a necessity.

Elisabeth C. Aiken currently teaches composition and literature at Saint Leo University.

Preface

The trade embargo imposed upon Cuba is a subject of particular interest to me. Until I embarked on this project, it had not been a subject discussed much in my circles of family and friends, yet it has always caught my attention, perhaps due to the apparent amount of effort that the United States government expends enforcing it. In particular, after the end of the Cold War and the demise of the Soviet Union, it appeared to me that this embargo, along with Fidel Castro, would soon disappear.

In 1996, political events led to the strengthening of the embargo, as Castro deftly manipulated the United States Congress into toughening a weakened Helms-Burton act. Castro accomplished this when his Cuban air force planes shot down two unarmed planes over international waters near Cuba. This event was followed in early 1998 by the historic visit of Pope John Paul II to Cuba, a visit that at that time was seen as a possible catalyst for fueling a transition toward democracy in Cuba, much like the Polish transition that had occurred in Poland a decade earlier. Unfortunately, for reasons too numerous and diverse to address here, that did not happen.

In the spring of 2002, several events happened that kept the trade embargo in my thoughts. Western Carolina University presented a speech by Lech Wałęsa, former president of Poland and a principal figure in that country's transition from communist rule to a free market capitalist society. In particular I was struck by the encouraging words of President Walesa as he compared the pre-transition events in Poland to current events in Cuba. In the following weeks there was a series of events receiving a lot of media coverage — most notably, President Bush's speech in Miami reaffirming an unwavering stance toward the embargo, and even more important, ex-president Jimmy Carter's visit to Cuba.

I have had an opinion for several years that the embargo was a failure, perhaps meant to serve the United States as a political tool, in order to serve our own self-interest while punishing the same innocent Cuban people it is purported to be trying to liberate. But this is just my opinion, based on my own beliefs, readings, and observations. How does the average Cuban feel?

In our small community in western North Carolina, I have repeatedly encountered Cubans living here. In my travels throughout the continental United States, Alaska and Canada, I have also encountered and engaged in conversation with many Cubans, as well as others with an apparent interest in Cuba, her people, and their well-being. These individuals are found in a wide variety of circumstances and professions from health care professionals to fishers, hotel clerks, and retirees. A quick, informal poll of these people indicated that there was a wide difference of opinion about the impact of the embargo.

My local library and the repository library at Western Carolina University hold several academic books about the embargo. I was able to use them as a starting point, but quickly found that they were mostly limited to analyzing the political, sociological or economic effects of the embargo on the Cuban economy, describing relations between Cuba and the United States, or, as I found in one, extolling the alleged virtues of living in a communist paradise. My main question, that of how this embargo affects the common Cuban, went unanswered.

The folks heard here within these pages are but a few examples of the voices of our history, of Cuba's history, of my history. This project started simply as an English paper, but with the encouragement and guidance of Professor Aiken and the English department at Western Carolina University it grew into a need to document this living history.

Initially I created a questionnaire and distributed it to many persons of Cuban descent and people simply having an interest in Cuban affairs. Those first responses led to in-depth interviews of five subjects. They ranged from a retired former equivalent of attorney general for Cuba, to a person who was perhaps the highest ranking dissident civilian at the Bay of Pigs fiasco, to American missionaries who have labored on the ground in Cuba. That was the inauspicious start of this project. The initial collection of material was sufficient for me, not in providing the answers I sought, but to fuel the desire to seek more people in the hopes of finding the answer to the one burning question of the embargo: "Why?"

Introduction

Over 45 years ago, on New Year's Day in 1959, the United States and Cuba unknowingly began a long decline in their relations. In Cuba, a series of events had led the dictator Fulgencio Batista to leave the island under the cover of darkness, clearing the path for the person who was supposed to have been the greatest Catholic patriot the young republic of Cuba had ever seen to come riding to her rescue, the long-anticipated and heralded arrival of a slightly disheveled man leading a small ragtag army of rebels, motivating them with his fiery rhetoric — Fidel Castro.

Within the following two to three years, this man, this supposed savior of his often proclaimed "beloved isle," birthed the greatest fears that had been gestating within the minds of his countrymen and women: he sold out. Not only did he sell out to the highest bidder, selling Cuba for the rewards that would enable him to continue to rule the island and her people, but he sold out to a nation whose actions and deeds had always managed to raise the wariness and suspicions of all those who had watched her, studied her, knew her, and feared her. Fidel Castro could not have come up with a worse highest bidder, save for the Chinese government, for that loathed and feared bidder was the Soviet Union. By the time Fidel Castro had assumed power and aligned with the communists, he had confirmed everyone's greatest fear, and change arrived in Cuba.

With these changes, these strict measures imposed on Cubans under the threat of death, Castro, emboldened, started nationalizing industries, buildings, farms, commerce and eventually even homes. Among these were properties, businesses, and homes belonging to many foreign nationals, including U.S. citizens. Castro continued to blatantly expropriate and confiscate, while United States ambassador Philip Bonsal kept reassuring Washington that a practical political solution was eminent. These measures rapidly progressed, along with an outcry from U.S. corporations, rising almost in tandem with incoming waves of Cuban refugees landing on U.S. soil.

Perhaps the most brazen of all appropriations was when Fidel Castro ordered the taking of oil refineries owned by ESSO and Shell. As pressure mounted, the United States government, under the leadership of President Dwight D. Eisenhower, was eventually left with no recourse but to impose economic sanctions upon Cuba, in August of 1960. With little fanfare, if any, the United States embargo on Cuba was born.

Although we tend to think of embargoes as modern political tools that can be used to reach an objective without military intervention, they are an almost timeless military strategy, having been first recorded in ancient Greece. Quite possibly they were in use ages before that. What we now call an embargo was then known as a siege. The main objective of a siege was to bring a targeted population — or, more likely, an opposing army — to its knees by cutting off all possible means of supplies. This objective is like the objective an embargo typically strives to accomplish. The difference is that rather than trying to subdue opposing armies, modern day embargoes attempt to subdue the political regimes that control those armies, and the subjects of nations or territories.

The embargo on Cuba was first implemented in 1960 in response to Fidel Castro's blatant anti-American stance, and has outlived most of the original players of this tragic drama, with Fidel Castro the noticeable exception. This political tool of the United States not only continues, but in 1996 was strengthened by Congress, thanks to senators Helms and Burton. The impasse created by the embargo is as strong as ever due to the incendiary rhetoric of President George W. Bush and Castro.

Throughout these decades a debate has been maintained within most political circles regarding the need and effectiveness of this policy. In recent times, this debate has grown, both within the exiled Cuban community and the U.S. population in general. Although the media provide coverage of trips to Cuba by prominent U.S. citizens, it usually ignores their message, delivering to our increasingly apathetic and uninformed population a bland interpretation of events. This was most noticeable in the trip by former president Jimmy Carter to Cuba in 2002. During this visit President Carter enjoyed unprecedented access to the Cuban people. His speech was not only uncensored, it was delivered live. Think about that for a moment. Here was Fidel Castro, an unrelenting communist dictator, known to oppress the Cuban people with a fist of steel, and he not only consented to allow President Carter unfettered access, but allowed him to meet with leading Cuban dissidents. It is difficult to imagine why Castro allowed this, but he did, and Carter made good use of this access.

The amazing aspect of this meeting is that it was allowed within the Cuban constitution. Its significance is the seed it planted in the Cuban mind. For decades these beautiful people have been under a harsh, oppressive rule, and have been led to believe that there were no options other than to wait for the death of Castro, followed by the collapse of his regime. Here in front of them, on live national (Cuban) TV was an American former president, standing next to their "president," Fidel Castro, informing them that not only was change possible, but that it could come from the Cuban people and their own constitution, a constitution which Castro himself had been on record swearing to uphold. Carter, a Nobel Peace Prize recipient and former peanut farmer, continues to plant. In this speech he planted not peanuts, but seeds of thought, change, and perhaps most importantly, hope.

"How did this happen?" you ask. You may recollect that visit not as one of importance, but instead as one during which Carter was presented once more as a naive liberal has been by the American media. The coverage of his speech was minimal. Yet the impact of his speech upon the Cuban population was historically significant. Carter had met with dissidents known as *opositores* (opposers). These brave souls have made the distinction that they are not dissenting from communist dogma, but opposing what they see as abuses of the Cuban constitution. They garnered over 11,000 signatures to call for a national referendum on the Cuban government. Castro, true to form, staged elaborate marches, with thousands of Cubans bussed in against their will, in an effort to quiet the growing murmur of debate and discontent. Ironically, Castro's speeches proposed using the same mechanism of referendum to establish that there would be no future need for referenda on the governing party's governance. His referendum would amend the Cuban constitution to recognize the Marxist-Leninist Communist Party of Cuba as the only party ever needed to govern.

As this heavy-handed, intimidating approach did not squelch the rumblings of dissent, Castro took a direct approach, one which he was more at ease implementing: he jailed the dissidents. Seventy-six dissidents were jailed, tried and sentenced with expediency typical of Castro's legal system, no defense allowed, no civil rights accorded to the accused, lest they may prove innocent. These seventy-six men and women were guilty of possessing "subversive material," books provided by the United States government and bibles sent by missionaries from the U.S. and many other countries, with the aim of establishing a small, intimate libraries in people's homes that would be accessible to the general public. Not much more controversial than what may reside in your home library. For this, sentences were imposed ranging from eight to twenty-six years for all but two of the dissidents. These two men received the ultimate sentence for their crime: death by firing squad at *el paredón* (the wall). They were allegedly guilty of hijacking a vessel in an attempt to flee this communist paradise and the repressive atmosphere of Castro's Cuba and reach the U.S.

It begs the question of what is more outrageous: that they were not allowed to present a defense, or that they had reached international waters and were forced to return to Cuba and certain death by none other than the U.S. Coast Guard under an agreement which was initially implemented by President Bill Clinton and continues to this day. America may be land of the free and the home of the brave, but if you are a Cuban and caught at sea, all bets are off. The United States will gladly take you back to Cuba, no questions asked. Furthermore, consider that the U.S. adheres to the policy that the embargo against Cuba must be kept in place as a means to punish Cuba for its human rights abuses. Yet fleeing Cubans, regardless of whether they are on a raft, boat, inner tube, or even swimming, are sent back to Cuba for prosecution by the Cuban government when they are intercepted by agents of the U.S. government at sea.

For the hundreds, if not thousands, of Cubans attempting to flee Cuba every year, the sea has become their own *paredón*, as evident by the empty makeshift rafts frequently found and documented by organizations such as *Hermanos al Rescate* (Brothers to the Rescue). Those Cubans who survive this brutal journey have to reach dry land to avoid being forcibly returned by the U.S. Coast Guard. The Cold War gave Eastern Europe the Berlin Wall and the Iron Curtain, representing ideological differences between the communist countries comprising the Soviet block and the progressive Western nations. Cuba's Iron Curtain, as physical as the Berlin Wall that separated East Germans from their friends and families in West Germany is a ninety-plus-mile expanse of turquoise waters.

The embargo impacts the lives of millions of Cubans, exiled or not.

In addition, the United States expends a great amount of money and effort enforcing this policy, with no apparent consideration of its real impact, as seen from a political, economic, social, or human rights perspective for the Cuban people.

A reason that this topic remains in the media, even in a diluted version, is because of its importance to Americans. Cuba is physically close to the U.S., approximately 90 miles due south of Key West, Florida. Exiled Cubans and Cuban Americans are a large, vocal, and politically active group based mostly in South Florida that endeavors to keep its issues present in the policies of the current administration. The majority of the exiled community appears to be evenly split between keeping the embargo versus dismantling it, yet the exiled political leadership has maintained a hard-line pro-embargo stance, as reflected in its unwavering support for any politician or policy that is anti-Castro.

A minority of the exiled leadership has voiced the need for dialogue and efforts toward dismantling the embargo. At the head of the list is the obvious argument that after 47 years, the embargo has not punished the Castro government, but has instead punished the innocent Cuban population while furthering Castro's regime. This is followed by strong evidence that the embargo has created a rift not only between exiled Cubans but also between them and Cubans on the island.

Recent interviews of members of the exiled community indicate a growing consensus that the embargo is a failure, as far as the general well-being of the Cuban people is concerned. If the embargo were to be lifted, events like those that happened in Eastern Europe would follow. While there is not a Berlin Wall to tear down, there is an impenetrable wall of political and human rights violations, and its dismantling would greatly benefit Americans and Cubans alike. But it is of political and economic interest for the U.S. government to keep the embargo in place. The United States has a huge investment in its military industry, and, as the self-anointed "sole super power" of the world, it would be to justify these enormous expenditures if we didn't have the rogue nation of Cuba sitting at our backdoor. These policies were much more evident during the Reagan Administration. Recent and current administrations furthered this siege mentality, evident by the recent Helms-Burton Act, President George W. Bush's speeches during his first term and during his re-election campaign stump speeches.

Introduction

The true intents of the U.S. government are seen suspiciously by some of the exiled Cuban leadership. A belief that the true purpose of the U.S. keeping the embargo in place is solely political permeates their thoughts. "All is negotiable: policies, embargo, immigration," Dr. Elpidio Perez says in an interview. He explains further:

> The United States do [sic] what they need to do as they see best for the United States. This is a practical country, run by practical people. Their true intents are state secrets, but they manipulate policies as needed. Whether returning rafters [people fleeing Cuba on makeshift rafts] or keeping them, condemning Castro or being silent and sending wheat, it is all intended to serve one purpose and that is to benefit the United States. If there is [sic] collateral benefits to Cubans without looking weak on Castro, then great. If there are none — then too bad.

Opposing exiled political leaders brave enough to be frank in their discussions will admit that the embargo, with its lack of true universal enforcement, is a failure. They also view the hard-line stance of the most vociferous anti-Castro groups to be counterproductive to the cause of returning democracy to Cuba. These groups are seen as single-mindedly intent on punishing Fidel Castro at all costs, without any regard for the general Cuban populace. These groups, well-funded and well-connected politically, are seen by the rest of the American nation as the authoritative voice for the exiled Cuban community. A search of Internet sites that belong to these groups confirms this, as they appear to promote any material that vilifies Castro or his regime, that denigrates dissenting opinions from the exiled community, and they do not offer a rational discussion or investigation of any dissenting arguments. Other Web sites, while offering a more rational approach to their pro-embargo stance, do not express any dissenting opinion. Web sites for any Cuban-American group that tolerates, discusses or promotes an anti-embargo argument are few and hard to find.

Yet there is a minority of the exiled Cuban leadership that does not maintain a hard-line pro-embargo approach, and appears to have no faith in it as a weapon to topple Castro. One of the more progressive exiled leaders, Alberto Martinez, proclaims:

> Cubans and Cuban-Americans, along with anyone else, [who] wait for the United States to solve the problem of Fidel Castro, are naïve

and possibly even idiots. Why have so many years gone by? Because the main weapon that the United States will use against Fidel Castro is time. Look at the once formidable Soviet Union. The United States did not engage it directly in military action, but indirectly through the Cold War, and basically just waited. The solution to Cuba's problem will come from Cubans, no one else. In fact, it *needs* to come from Cubans. All this meddling by the United States does no more than ignite those volatile emotions for which we Cubans are famous. It will be of grave consequence for the Cuban people to not engage in any and all opportunities of dialogue between the communities, because when the time arrives that Fidel Castro is gone, we may have a civil war instead of a peaceful transition. And *that* should weigh heavily on the collective consciousness of the United States.

It appears that while the majority anti-Castro, pro-embargo leadership has the funds and abilities to continue influencing U.S. policies toward Cuba, this is a misguided effort that could lead to serious consequences. The idea of dialogue and trade as the weapons of choice is slowly gaining momentum and they appear to be the tactics most likely to succeed in the quest for a peaceful transition toward Cuban democracy. The task at hand will be to educate both the exiled community and the political leadership in Washington, D.C. so that this transition may happen. These efforts need to take place while encouraging a more rational dialogue among Cubans, without the virulent rhetoric, but with a tone of understanding and practicality, maintaining focus on the most desirable prize: a peaceful transition in Cuba toward a democratic state.

I

Cuba Up to Fidel Castro

Cuba is a young nation, barely past 100 years since her independence from Spain, with almost half of those years lived in the dark recesses of Fidel Castro's dictatorship. Cuba's history prior to Castro is fascinating, complicated and extensive. I will summarize this period in this chapter, as there exist many books presenting this topic in greater detail. The island of Cuba perhaps came about as a result of an impact of an asteroid, an event that created the Caribbean basin and its isles as proposed by the Alvarez theory. The island was originally inhabited by three distinct indigenous peoples: the Ciboney, the Tainos, and the Guanajatabeyes. All three appeared to subsist primarily on fishing and agriculture, and they coexisted on fragile terms. The largest of these groups, the Tainos, had crops that included corn, squash, yams and beans. Skilled weavers, they created products ranging from enclosure nets for aquaculture, to hammocks for sleeping. These were the first known users, hence probable inventors, of the hammock, one of the few surviving legacies from these populations. The Tainos were also distinguished by their use of tobacco in a social context, and their belief in a supernatural being and life after death.

The indigenous people, hammocks and Cuba were introduced to the Europeans when Christopher Columbus accidentally discovered the island on October 28, 1942, during his famed initial voyage. Columbus initially named the Island "Juana" to honor the daughter of his benefactors, King Ferdinand V and Isabella I of Spain. The island was renamed several times by Columbus, eventually acquiring its current name, Cuba. I find it fitting that the name that stuck was one derived from the name given by the original inhabitants, Cubanacan. The source of Cuba's nickname is unknown, but most likely from the Spaniards who realized that Cuba was *la Perla del Caribe*, the Pearl of the Caribbean, a most important jewel in the Queen's crown of colonies.

Cuban Exiles on the Trade Embargo

The island was not settled by Europeans until 1511, when a Spanish soldier, Diego Velasquez, established the town of Baracoa, followed by other settlements, including Santiago de Cuba (1514) and Havana (1515). Cuba was found to be rich in natural bounty, and rapidly became transformed by the Spanish into a key location to support and supply their exploration and empire building efforts in Florida, Mexico, and beyond. Within the isle, the Spaniards established and developed plantations and mines. These and other factors, coupled with the introduction of viruses and diseases, led to the rapid decline and eventual extinction of the aboriginal populations. By the mid 1500s, these once friendly people were all but gone, and were rapidly replaced as a labor source by imported African slaves, later supplemented with cheap Asian laborers.

Cuba prospered through the 16th and 17th centuries, despite repeated assaults and hardships provoked by pirates, buccaneers, and naval forces of enemy nations. Trade regulations and restrictions imposed upon Cuba by Spain were largely ignored and not enforced by the colonists, fostering a population growth that swelled to over 500,000 at the dawn of the 1800s. Spain's iron-fisted, imperialistic grip on Cuba began to show signs of weakness during the 1830s and 1840s as the colonist Cubans organized and revolted against the despotic rule of governor Capitán Manuel Tacón. These initial revolts were frequently quelled, often in a brutal manner. The island experienced movements calling for independence, as well as calls for annexation into the United States (1848–1851), multiple purchase offers from the U.S., and then a declared independence in 1868 leading to the Ten Years War, all of which exacted a high cost financially and in lost lives for both Spain and Cuba.

The end of the Ten Years' War in 1878 led to important concessions granted to Cubans by Spanish authorities. This was followed by the abolition of slavery in 1886, the halting of imported cheap Chinese labor in 1871, and the proclamation of equality among people regardless of race in 1893. Spain, much as a wife beater who claims to have reformed, only to again eventually strike his wife again, was unwilling or unable to allow Cuba to continue to thrive independently and renewed oppressive measures which led again to revolt — the famed *Grito de Yara* (Yell of Yara) on February 24, 1895. This was the revolution that introduced the world to the famed Cuban poet and hero José Martí, along with General Máximo Gómez y Báez. The intervention of the United States in this conflict ignited the Spanish-American War, and occasioned the sinking of the USS Maine in Havana's harbor on February 15, 1898, which further intensified the resolve and commitment of U.S. involvement. The war ceased on December 10, 1898, with a treaty signed by the United States and Spain, with Spain conceding defeat, resigning sovereignty over Cuba, and most significantly, allowing the U.S. to rule the island until the initial independent Cuban government was installed on May 20, 1902.

The installation of the initial government under the presidency of Tomás Estrada Palma was not without controversy, for in the original Cuban constitution written and adopted in 1901, the United States was assured a continued role as provided through an overbearing legislative act delineating the imperialist tendencies of the U.S. toward Cuba. The coerced passage of the Platt Amendment allowed the United States to intervene at its discretion, including through use of its military, in Cuban government affairs. The U.S. squelched several uprisings in Cuba through 1912, protecting the heavy investments and control of US corporate interests in the island's sugar cane industry and national economy. These uprisings had resulted mostly from great dissatisfaction with a government riddled with ongoing fraud and corruption.

In September 1906, under the cover of the Platt Amendment, the U.S. took control of the Republic of Cuba through a military intervention that lasted until 1912. There were some positive aspects to these interventions, as yellow fever was eradicated, and an initial investment in infrastructure was accomplished. Eventually, late in 1912, the election of Mario García Menocal returned the Conservative Party to power, thus also returning a relative calm to the island that lasted through Cuba's entry with the Allies into World War I.

The suffocating grip of U.S. corporate entities upon Cuba and her financial, agricultural, and industrial sectors continued in an unrelenting manner in the period following World War I. This suffocation of the Cuban people introduced a sense of doom and crisis, leading to the election of Gerardo Machado y Morales of the Liberal Party in November 1924, on the platform of promised reform. The rallying cries against the imperialist notions of the United States, from someone who had draped himself in the cloth of a nationalist Cuban savior, would later be seen and felt repeatedly, most notably with Fidel Castro in 1959. By his second term, Gerardo Machado y Morales had sunk Cuba economically, with failed loans from abroad and misguided economic policies at home, while establishing a dictatorship that brutally suppressed the slightest opposition. His playbook must be one that Castro obtained and has followed, except for the final chapter: in August 1933 the Cuban army supported a general uprising which succeeded in forcing Machado's exile abroad.

Yet, for Cubans the following years must have seemed a dream gone bad, for the government frequently changed, usually with a violent coup, thereby violence and unrest dominated. During these times, Cubans awaited the United States to exercise its "right" as deeded by the Platt Amendment, but an intervention never materialized. Instead, the Platt Amendment was abrogated, as the U.S. attempted to impose other measures designed to alleviate or suppress the unrest. This spiral was stabilized to a certain degree with the impeachment of President Miguel Mariano Gomez by a Cuban Senate mostly controlled by Fulgencio Batista Zaldívar. The former head of the army, Federico Laredo Brú, was installed as president, and, with the Senate's blessing, initiated a series of social and economic measures designed to institute reform. In 1940 the election of Batista as president, along with the propagation of a new constitution, appeased the restlessness of the Cuban populace and diminished political tensions.

In December 1941, following the horrific Japanese attack on Pearl Harbor, Cuba declared war on Japan, Germany, and Italy. The elections of 1944 saw the losing candidate of four years earlier return, this time with a broad coalition of support that led to victory. The presidency of Ramón Grau San Martín enjoyed the fruits of the 1941 war declaration, as it facilitated Cuba's charter membership in the United Nations in 1945, but that was perhaps the only highlight of his administration. Food shortages and an abundance of crises plagued his term. A surge in popularity, fueled by negotiated sugar prices and concessions from US industries favorable to Cuban growers, were not sufficient to keep him in office. Carlos Prio Socarrás, a former cabinet minister, was elected president in June 1948. Once again, though, Cuba was denied a peaceful transition into a democratic era, as inflation rose, despite efforts to contain it, and with it the cost of living, political unrest and violence.

Fulgencio Batista Zaldívar, supported by the Cuban army, returned in March 1952 to grasp power again. Batista installed a series of changes designed to return Cuba to a state dominated by one: a dictatorship. He suspended the constitution of 1940, disbanded Cuba's Congress, and promised free elections by the fall of 1954, while installing a provisional government. The only significant challenge to Batista occurred in 1953 when a young lawyer fomented an uprising in the eastern province of Oriente. Batista was easily able to crush Fidel Castro's initial challenge, further cementing his control and power in the months leading to the elections of 1954. These elections went smoothly, at least for Batista. Heavy handed, repressive tactics caused his repeat opponent from 1940, Ramón Grau San Martín, to withdraw from the election, citing terrorist persecution by Batista's supporters under the direction of Batista himself. With his sole opponent gone into exile in the U.S., Batista coasted to an easy victory and was once again installed as president on February 24, 1955.

Batista's election and return as president was accompanied by the return of constitutional rule, amnesty for political prisoners, and the release of Castro from prison. Castro decided to leave the island, seeking exile in the United States initially, before settling as an exile in Mexico. With Batista's government came a return to the fraud and corruption of times past, although this was largely tolerated by the Cuban people, as installed economic reform policies, along with stabilized global markets and sugar prices, created an era of economic prosperity and political stability.

The return of Castro, with an invading army of 80-odd men, must have seemed like an omen that the political and economic stability was to be short-lived. Castro's invading forces were easily defeated and captured by Batista's army, but Castro himself managed to escape into the mountains where he was able to reorganize and initiate guerrilla tactics against the Batista government. Castro was able to gain the trust and support of the Cuban public, proclaiming himself to be the great savior of his nation, there to defeat a corrupt and centrist government, with no intentions of governing himself, just willing to return political power to its true owners: the people of Cuba. Fidel Castro was wisely able to parlay this facade into a revolt that swelled in support and momentum, most notably from a general revolt he called on March 17, 1958, until the collapse of the Batista government. Batista resigned and fled the island on January 1, 1959.

In mid-February of 1959, Fidel Castro, the young lawyer with the previously declared lack of want of political office, a man raised in the

Catholic faith, educated in the finest Catholic school in Cuba, the product of an amorous liaison between a Cuban servant and a Spaniard, the self-declared savior of Cuba, was installed as premier, plunging Cuba and its people into a long, ongoing era of hardship, death, and misery.

II

Castro's Cuba

New Year's Day, 1959. A time of celebration, rejoicing and fear. The government of Batista had seeming collapsed overnight; Fulgencio Batista had resigned and fled from Cuba into exile. A new year, a new government. Change was in the air. Some hearts were light with joy and exuberance, others were heavy, laden with fear and unrest.

Property owners in Cuba, as in other Hispanic countries, as well as Spain, favored masonry walls, typically covered with stucco. This kind of wall has several names, including *Paredón*. In the urban centers of Cuba, the exterior walls of homes, usually frosted with layers of stucco, march right up to the edge of the street. The *Paredón*, along with these exterior walls, would be called into service by Fidel Castro's forces in what would be a inauspicious distinction.

In the eastern city of Santiago de Cuba, Gabriel Muncia Gonzalez and Filiberto Torres López, along with Ramón Becerra in Cienfuegos, Ángel M. Clausell García in the capital of La Habana, and Armando Casola Sardaña in the westernmost province of Pinar de Rios, shared a common destiny in January 1959: all were victims of *El Paredón*. These men, in scenes often repeated throughout Cuba, were initiated into what would become Fidel Castro's preferred method of controlling past, present and future, real or imagined, and individuals who either actively opposed his regime, or simply did not want to participate in it.

In this manner, many men found their ultimate fate at the hands of the revolutionaries. They were torn from homes, ripped from the embraces of their loved ones, and forced to stand blindfolded, as they heard three last words. Hearts pounding, palms sweating, some grieved for the pain and suffering that they knew would come for their loved ones, while others remained stoic and heroic in the face of death. Cool tropical winter breezes carried the same words throughout the island repeatedly, over five hundred times in the early weeks of the revolutionaries' command and control of Cuba, under Fidel Castro. *Listos!* (Ready!) *Apunten!* (Aim!) *Fuego!* (Fire!) The explosive sound of volley after volley roared from rifles in front of property walls, in front of *El Paredón*.

The installation of Castro as premier in mid–February 1959, and his command of the revolutionaries and their firing squads, confirmed what had been predicted by some, ignored by others, and feared by most. It became increasingly evident to Cuba and the world that a difficult period lay ahead for most Cubans, as Castro's leftist tendencies quickly materialized.

Foreign corporations, mostly from the United States, and, in particular, sugar producers, became increasingly concerned in those early years as Castro implemented agrarian reforms that favored food crop production over sugar cane crops. This tension was heightening as Castro introduced laws that led to the prohibition of ownership of plantations by non-Cuban stockholders. Yet even rightful, law-abiding Cubans were not to escape this madness, as righteous men such as Enrique Anacleto Larrauri, saw his productive and prosperous fields of *henequén* (hemp, grown for its strong natural fibers used to make rope and other products) taken "for the good of the revolution," in exchange for worthless stock and the empty promise of a managerial position if he cooperated. As the appropriation of property grew in momentum, so did the "brain drain," as most of Cuba's educated professionals fled for the United States and elsewhere.

In 1960, the United States, under the presidency of Dwight D. Eisenhower, imposed initial trade sanctions in response to expropriations by the Castro regime of an estimated $1 billion in properties owned by U.S. corporations. The birth of tit-for-tat response and counter response grew to a crescendo, culminating in the complete severance of diplomatic relation between the two countries in January 1961, followed by the Bay of Pigs invasion on April 17, 1961, by anti-Castro exiles trained and supported by the United States. This invasion, also known to Cubans as the invasion of *Playa Girón* (Girón Beach), failed, as the invading exiled Cuban forces found their promised aerial support withdrawn at the last moment by President John F. Kennedy, an event that led to the capture, imprisonment and death of most of these brave souls.

It has been proposed by some of the individuals interviewed in this book that these events happened as Castro sold out quickly to the highest bidder, in a bidding competition that the United States self-righteously decided not to enter. Castro had approached the U.S. government with his hat in his hand, only to be treated as a pariah was told that President Eisenhower had no time for him, being too busy playing golf in Augusta, and that he would be allocated 15 minutes with Vice-President Richard Nixon. Those fifteen minutes, Castro was instructed, were the only access he would have to the U.S. government, so he "better use them well." That humiliating heavy-handed approach occasioned Castro's return to Havana with "his tail between his legs," his wounded pride leading to a further resolve to consecrate his position with the other bidder, the Soviet Union. This and other events were the decisive rolls of the dice with which the fate of Cuba was gambled away. Events had been set in motion prior to, and quickly thereafter, the fall of Batista, during which Castro employed smoke and mirrors tactics to evaluate which of the two superpowers would support and finance his ambitions to control and remain in power for as long as he lived. The third possible superpower of the time Castro quickly dismissed, for the Chinese he despised and saw as a nation of substandard people, a nation incapable of technological advances, a nation that did not possess the technology that he desired. The Soviets anted up to Castro's demands, while the United States idly stood by, convinced that Fidel would see the errors of his way, and come around begging for assistance. Castro had only to look as far as some as his neighbors to see that as the United States gives, it takes away, as in the changing regimes of Panama, Nicaragua, Guatemala and elsewhere. The Soviets had also employed the same tactics, but Castro apparently felt that he could control Soviet desires for involvement and dominance of Cuba in a manner that was most beneficial to him, something that he must have sensed would not happen if the United States won the bidding game.

The leaders of the Soviet Union must have salivated at the idea of controlling a location as strategic as Cuba. Less than a hundred miles from U.S. soil, the location was ideally situated to launch and expand their empire into Latin America and the Caribbean, much like the Spaniards had done 4½ centuries prior. The stage was set on the same scene, but the main characters had changed. The colonizing Spaniards had only ill-equipped indigenous populations to conquer, but now the Soviets had a formidable and eventually insurmountable obstacle: the force, might and resolve of the United States.

Soviet influence in Cuba was inevitable once Fidel Castro acceded to the Kremlin. Military support and equipment flooded the country, as did other military technology. In the fall of 1962, the United States became aware that the Soviet Union was installing missile sites on the island. A subsequent naval blockade of the island by President Kennedy raised tensions to unforeseen levels, but was needed to deny the Soviets continued shipments of military hardware to Cuba. The threat of nuclear war with the Soviet Union and Cuba shrouded tense days, as negotiations between Washington and the Kremlin were nervously held. On October 28, 1963, Soviet Premier Nikita Khrushchev agreed to, and eventually accomplished, the dismantling and removal of the missile sites and their related equipment, as a direct result of these high-level meetings. For its part, the United States agreed to concessions, including that it would no longer support or allow the exiled Cuban community to prepare for or undertake any future attempts to invade the island. Once again the astuteness of Castro was seen, as he was able to manipulate the United States into a decision that would allow him to maintain his unrelenting grasp on power in Cuba. This was a scene that would often be repeated in the future, as Castro would stage incidents carefully designed to influence decision makers in Washington, DC, while feigning indifference or opposite desires.

Tensions between Cuba and the United States remained elevated, and hostilities continued during the 1960s and beyond. Despite this, and with the help and support of the Swiss Embassy in Cuba, the U.S. and Cuba agreed in 1965 to allow Cuban nationals to migrate to the United States, if they desired to do so. By the time the last flight arrived in Miami in 1973, more than a quarter of a million Cubans had opted to leave. This was not a simple decision or task to undertake, for those who applied to leave immediately found themselves without work, without any means of income, while facing enormous difficulties just trying to provide the sustenance needed for them and their families to live, as they waited for permission to leave. Since Castro had decreed that all possessions belonged to the Cuban people, with the caveat that these possessions had to remain under his watch, persons applying to leave the island were forced out of their homes, their belongings taken without compensation, with not much more than a simple suitcase, at best, with a few meager possessions in hand, on the day they were actually able to flee. Cuban professionals were the bulk of this initial exodus, gladly trading professions as doctors, lawyers, and the like, for the opportunity to wash dishes, sweep the floors of diners, or do any meager task that paid, in a foreign country, with a foreign language, but with the promise of the ultimate American dream: freedom.

During this period, Castro labored greatly to export his revolution to Latin America, for which he managed to have Cuba expelled from Organization of American States (OAS) in 1962. Castro quickly alienated himself and Cuba from these countries while attempting to spread his brand of communism. The capture and execution of his closest aide, Che Guevara, in Bolivia, while training and leading a guerrilla movement in 1967, was rightly noted and upheld as proof by his accusers.

At home in Cuba, Castro continued to implement changes to solidify his power. The island's six provinces were divided into 14, from which a National Assembly was "elected" in the mid-1970s. The first congress of the Cuban Communist Party was held in 1975, following which the newly elected National Assembly held its first session, not surprisingly choosing Castro as the head of state.

Fidel Castro's disastrous domestic policies occasioned increased heavy dependence on the Soviet Union for funding and imports. The early 1970s saw the forgiveness or deferment of Cuba's debt by the Soviet bloc, as pacts were signed between the countries. Ironically, the 1970s also saw Cuba reenter the global community, as trade restrictions between members of the OAS and Cuba were formally ended at the OAS conference in 1975.

The United State eased travel restrictions during this time, and relations between the two countries began to improve, leading to the opening of offices in each other's capitals. Further warming of relations were never to materialize, as the U.S. rightly insisted that claims for nationalized properties must first be resolved, and that Cuba must cease or drastically reduce its attempts to export revolution notably, during that period, to Africa. But as an easing of restrictions would mean an easing of his grasp on the collective neck of the Cuban people, Castro managed to keep sanctions in place, as he not only increased activities in Africa, but also exported his hellacious brand of revolution to the Middle East country of Yemen.

Closer to home, Latin America and the Caribbean Basin countries were not spared his attention, as Castro continued to export his indoctrinating brand of communism to countries such as Nicaragua and El Salvador, often under a pretext of humanitarian missions, providing doctors and medical assistance, as well as educators. Once again, Castro's elaborate farce was exposed to the world when hundreds of Cuban advisors, soldiers and workers had to abruptly leave the island nation of Granada when the United States invaded in October 1983. In 1980, the United States suffered from Castro's manipulative attempts, as he poisoned the Mariel exodus with criminals and mental patients released from prisons and forced to travel to the U.S. along with true exile seekers. The truly humanistic attempt by the United States to accept a wave of mostly blue-collar exile seekers was marred by subsequent horrific acts committed by some of these individuals in the U.S. Eventually most of the criminals were secured and deported, although, in typical fashion, following another long game of cat and mouse politics with Castro. While Castro's true motive to contaminate this wave of exiles with these undesirable individuals may never be known, it is interesting to note again that this was an exodus of mostly blue-collar, working-class individuals, fleeing the alleged "worker's paradise" marketed by Castro and his regime to the rest of the world.

Relations between the Cuban government and the Kremlin also continued in cat and mouse fashion, as Castro accepted what he desired, and avoided what he perceived as a threat to weakening his control, to insure the continued survival of Marxist communist ideology. With one hand Castro rejected proposed economic and political changes presented by the Soviet Union, while with the other he signed a twenty-five year friendship treaty in 1989, with generous trade and financial support to Cuba.

This much needed financial support tendered by the Soviet Union would be short-lived, as the end of the Cold War and the subsequent collapse of the Soviet Union forced its member states, including Russia, to attend to domestic challenges and crises as they struggled to survive. Cuba's economy plunged in this era of increasing despair and emergency, fueled not only by the implosion of the Soviet Union and the withdrawal of Soviet troops and aid, but also catalyzed by the increased tightening of the embargo by the United States again. The dire economic situation in Cuba brought about an increasingly discontent populace, fanning the flames of hope that a change from within was at hand for Cuba. Once again, however, Castro was able to deftly suppress and control the Cuban people, although a tide of economic refugees left by any means possible.

The late 1990s might best be described as a schizophrenic period in the relationship between the United States and Fidel Castro's regime. The sinking by the Cuban Coast Guard of a hijacked Cuban ferry attempting to leave the island, and the horrendous loss of life, led to massive and unprecedented demonstrations. Castro once again befuddled those who try to predict his reactions, allowing all those who wished to leave free exit, although at the usual price of loss of possessions and jobs. The United States, unable or unwilling to see that the policies of its embargo were behind the wave of these economic refugees, in effect making them political refugees, decided to detain and arriving or intercepted Cubans as economic refugees, not as political asylum seekers, reversing the long held policy of granting asylum to all Cubans who fled. Over 30,000 Cubans intercepted at Sea were taken to refugee camps at the United States Guantánamo Naval Base in Cuba or to other refugee camps in Panama. Eventually the crisis was resolved, at least for the U.S. as it agreed to provide 20,000 refugees with visas annually. Further convoluting policies, the U.S. Coast Guard employed large-volume water hoses to refugees within yards of their setting foot on American soil, in an attempt to confine them and return them to Cuba. The Bill Clinton Administration had negotiated a semblance of truce, by agreeing with Cuba that any Cuban found at sea would be returned to Castro's regime, while those who managed to reach the U.S. would be allowed to stay and be processed through the Krome Detention Center outside of Miami, Florida, as part of the 20,000 entry visas agreement. Close did not count in this game of life and death; provided that the refugee survived the treacherous journey on the makeshift rafts, they either *had* to tag home plate, or faced certain return to Cuba. To be returned would be nothing like a return to the dugout or the showers, but much worse, a fate that made the possibility of death on the high seas worth risking for countless fleeing Cubans. It is incredible to realize that the United States had become, in effect, an extension of Cuba's Coast Guard, and further that it was willing to return individuals to a country with an extensive record of human rights abuses, abuses that forcibly returned refugees would certainly suffer upon arrival back in Cuba.

All is not roses and sunshine in Fidel Castro's Cuba. There are dissidents, vociferous and active as they can be, given the Castro's oppressive regime. These brave men and women are mostly united in the common cause of bringing democratic change to Cuba, with its inherent benefits that are taken for granted by U.S. citizens, including freedom. Freedom of expression, of assembly, to move about the country, to think, write, work, live as you see fit. All of these and more are denied to all Cubans. These dissidents have been jailed; they have endured torture, sham trials, and long sentences; many have made the ultimate sacrifice, life. Why? For simply expressing opposing views and desires different than those required by the ruling party and by Castro. Most of these men and women are advocates of a peaceful transition, of nonviolent means to achieve their goal of democracy and freedom, not unlike those exemplified by Martin Luther King, Jr. Many of these brave souls are members of the Concilio Cubano, a coalition boasting more than 100 dissident groups within Cuba that seek true political reform. Members of these groups are routinely harassed or worse, as noted above. In the early weeks of 1996, Cuban authorities detained or arrested over 150 of these individuals, one of the largest crackdowns since the infancy of the revolution.

Later that year, Cuban jet fighters shot down two unarmed civilian airplanes from the U.S., killing all of those onboard. The incident clearly occurred over international waters. These planes were part of the humanitarian mission of a Cuban exiles' organization called *Hermanos al Rescate* (Brothers to the Rescue), dedicated to acting as spotters for rafters fleeing the island, in an effort to increase the odds faced by refugees as they attempt to survive the crossing and reach land. Once a raft with people on board are spotted, these brave volunteers report the locations to the U.S. Coast Guard. Fidel Castro has stated that he did not give the order to shoot down the planes, a much-disputed assertion, as in the weeks prior to the downing he had commented on several occasions that he had given a directive to the Cuban air force to shoot down any civilian aircraft that violated Cuban airspace.

These incidents may appear to have been isolated, were it not for the fact that the U.S. Congress was engaged at that time with debating the merits of the proposed Helms-Burton Act, a law that would formalize and strengthen the U.S. embargo on Cuba. Brought before Congress by Senators Helms and Burton at the directive of the powerful Republican Cuban-American lobby, the Act's provisions had been diluted by Congress in the days leading to the vote on its passage into law. Just prior to final vote, the act regained all of its provisions as Congress reacted with outrage, in particular to the downing of the two civilian aircraft, and the narrow escape of a third plane.

Why, in a country such as Cuba — where all is monitored, and not a thing, least of all the downing of unarmed civilian aircraft, occurs without the knowledge of Fidel Castro — did such incidents occur just prior to the passage of the diluted act? That passage would have eased the trade sanctions, such as those theatrically demanded by Castro on a regular basis. Once again, it appeared that Castro had manipulated the United States to take a course of action that on the surface seemed unwanted by Castro, and was rallied against by Castro as further proof of American imperialist desires, but, if studied closely, was seen to benefit Castro's perpetual need to remain securely in power. The reinforced Helms-Burton Act provided Castro with ammunition to justify to Cubans and the world his oppressive measures and provided an excuse for his failed economic policies, while he clothed himself again in nationalist fervor. For example, without the embargo, Castro could not continue to oppress and dominate the population employing such tactics as the *libreta de racionamiento* (food ration card), mandated since 1960. Controlling the food supply to the hungry Cuban nation assures control of the nation. Some members of the global community have fallen for this, and decry the embargo as the chief cause of Cuba's woes, including nations allied with the United States, such as Mexico and Spain. Pope John Paul II, on the other hand, spoke in Cuba, reprimanding Castro for continuing to use the embargo as an excuse for his failed economic policies, while also using it as an excuse to oppress Cubans in general and dissenters in particular, negating any hope for true political reform.

The Helms-Burton Act made the economic embargo of Cuba permanent. Since 1960 the embargo had been mostly a directive renewed yearly by the U.S. president. Other provisions of the legislation sought to make it more difficult for foreign companies, investors and governments to trade with Cuba if they "derived benefits" from property worth more than $50,000 that had been confiscated from U.S. citizens. These citizens included Cuban-American exiles in South Florida whose lobbying efforts brought the act into law. These provisions within the Helms-Burton Act have had to be suspended every six months by the president, as required within the law itself. This occurred as Mexico, England, Spain and the rest of the European Union accused the United States of attempting to export its policies to the world through this act. This portion of the act bars any ship or business that enters a Cuban port, or transacts in commerce with a Cuban entity, from doing the same for six months with the

United States, its citizens and corporations. In effect, this serves to isolate not Cuba, but the United States from the rest of world, as Cuba's largest trading and investing countries are Mexico and Canada, followed by England, Japan, and the European Union.

The Helms-Burton Act in its final aggressive form has served Fidel Castro well. Following its passage, the Central Committee of Cuba's Communist Party met in full session to implement new measures relative to the act. That this occurred in a full session is notable since in the entire length of Castro's dictatorship a full session had only been convened five times. Using the act as an attempt to justify their actions, the Committee quickly authorized more oppressive measures directly aimed toward dissenters, intellectuals, and those rare Cuban businesses that had been allowed to experimentally engage in trade with foreign companies. The Committee charged individuals with engaging in subversive efforts to undermine Cuba's economy and ideology, leading to vows by Castro to increase efforts to squelch these traitors of "the cause" and to increase measures engineered to assure compliance. Once again, the embargo had been manipulated and employed by Castro and his regime to their benefit, entrenching Castro's position further.

III

Echenique

"This is politics, not truth." A simple statement made by a simple man. In the midst of our conversation about the embargo imposed on Cuba by the United States, this statement speaks volumes with its simplicity, much as the greatness of this man is exemplified through his own simplicity. Alberto Martinez Echenique epitomizes the contemporary exiled Cuban hero. A man of 75, he is quiet, thin and deeply tanned by the harsh South Florida sun and previously by the equally harsh and unrelenting Cuban sun.

Echenique, as he prefers to be called, is an honest man, a person who will look you straight in the eye through his silver wire-rimmed glasses, and speak the truth as he knows it, a habit that has endangered his life in Cuba and elsewhere. I have known this man since I was a child. More accurately, this man has known me since my birth, for he is a great friend of my family and a past business associate of my father. This man has labored in the construction industry since arriving from Cuba, a physically demanding profession in the hot, humid Florida climate. He has also worked for an assortment of local governmental agencies, and continues to display an incredible work ethic despite his years. This is a humble man, a person who believes in and dedicates himself to church, family, and community, a quietly passionate blue-collar individual, unafraid of putting his shoulder to the task, and yet just as intellectual, intelligent, and ambitious as any entrepreneur.

Echenique has approached living in exile in the United States in the same manner as you or I would approach a chore that has to be done: not necessarily an unpleasant one, not necessarily pleasurable, either, but just another task. He is at once grateful for the opportunities provided to him in this nation, while longing for Cuba, much like the faithful await the return of their savior. This quiet, under the radar approach to subsisting in the United States is so deceptive. Here is a great man who was known as one of Fidel Castro's harshest critics even before January 1959, yet if you were to pass Echenique on the dynamic, crowded sidewalks of Little Havana in Miami, you would probably not give him a second glance. If on a hot Miami afternoon you went searching for him among a group of Cubans playing dominoes at a park in Calle Ocho, you would be hard-pressed to distinguish him from the other participants. Which one is this man of inner strength? Which one could he be?

Perhaps after studying such a group carefully you would detect him, not from a description provided to you by anyone, but by his values: honesty, righteousness, and fairness. Added to this mix is a graciousness and charisma, not poured on like a small-town southern politician, but graceful and subtle. He pulls you into his realm and has you hanging on his every word, delivered in a manner so plain and factual that you could easily miss the great truths embodied in them.

Echenique has spent 46 of his 75 years in the United States. When asked why he left Cuba, he replies by explaining the events that led to his being branded an enemy of the Cuban state. Echenique knew Fidel Castro in Belén, his high school, a Catholic school run by Jesuit priests. These priests kept cattle, hogs and other large animals for which Echenique's father provided veterinary care and services. Echenique vividly remembers that Castro, a couple of years ahead of him, was already known as a "hothead." At home, around the dinner table on the days that his father tended to the priests' stock, an increasingly familiar theme would emerge. Echenique's father would comment on Castro's growing notoriety, including his frequent verbal assaults and misstatements directed at anyone who happened to be present. These appeared to serve no purpose other than to establish him as someone who was not well liked, as someone would look for any excuse to cause trouble, therefore as someone who would frequently be found gracing the director's offices or school infirmary as a result of a altercation. Echenique's father would marvel at how Castro would continuously repeat this cycle, suffering the consequences from the director of the school or the beatings served upon him by his peers, and like a stubborn ass, would go at it again.

In the 1950's Echenique attended the University of Havana where he studied economics. It was during this time that he was beginning to be noticed by his fellow classmates and student leaders as an honest, sincere, politically ambitious young man. It was this ambition — this need to speak out and make his views, convictions, and truth known — that became a driving force that eventually led to launching him as a radio and television commentator. Echenique became fully immersed in politics, on and off campus, became involved in the student government, and rapidly rose in prominence while sparring verbally with Castro at every opportunity. "Castro was then a great threat to the nation of Cuba, to his countrymen and women," Echenique says. This relentless drive to speak the truth led to Echenique to eventually leave the University of Havana and transfer to the Catholic school, Santo Tomas de Villanova, as the University of Havana was being overrun by communist sympathizers.

Echenique explains, "Even on the university campus, before he headed off to the mountains for his revolution, Castro was already seen as a threat to Cubans and a communist sympathizer. His brother Raul was very involved with the communist student organizations and the Communist Party, of which Fidel Castro made an effort to appear as tolerant of, but not a sympathizer of, let alone a believer of their dogma. I took every opportunity to attempt to expose Fidel for the 'hidden communist' he was at that time; I attacked him on the radio and television."

"Once Batista fell, I had to go into hiding, for I knew I was high on the list as an enemy of Castro, and would have been taken to *el paredon* and shot, if captured. I was eventually able to flee the island and headed initially to Tampa, Florida, where my in-laws had previously established themselves."

In the United States, Echenique was unable to resume his university studies, having the responsibilities of a growing family. Yet, despite the pressures of life and work, he continued to be active politically within the exiled Cuban community, satisfying a need that is entrenched in him even to this day. It was this deep conviction, this sense of responsibility toward his country, his family and his friends, which led to his return to Cuba in the early 1960s as a member of the invading forces at the Bay of Pigs.

Within Echenique there exists a vast capacity for love, as demonstrated by his love for Cuba. This love for his homeland is such, that with three small children at home, one of them just a newborn, he packed and headed off to participate with the brigade of Cuban exiles, *Brigada 2506*. He left a wife and family who not only loved and needed him, but supported him. His wife provided him with reassurance and encouragement, reinforcing his belief that the right decision had been made, even if it could lead to the ultimate sacrifice.

Echenique's deeply furrowed face freely displays his emotions as he speaks of the past he has experienced and survived. He was present at the Bay of Pigs invasion, returning not as a soldier, not as a politician, and definitely not as a bystander, but as a patriot, ready to reclaim his homeland from the tyrannical grasp of Castro and his regime. As Echenique relates his experiences, his voice remains smooth as the soothing tropical breezes that caress the Cuban coast in the evenings, yet his eyes moisten and relax as he appears to look back into his history, a history as fresh to him as this morning's cup of Cuban coffee. His words carry a great sense of sorrow as he speaks about that day: "It was a travesty, perhaps the greatest tragedy brought upon the Cuban people, for here we [were] on the beach, vastly outnumbered by Castro's troops, yet we [were] winning ..." Here his voice betrays his emotions, but this is quickly reigned in, and he continues, apparently unaware of this telling moment, "We were beating them easily. Easily!"

Echenique's voice and face become enlivened in such a manner that carries me with him, back to that fateful day of over 44 years — and many, many tears — ago. I can feel the pain in him. It is there as plain as the Guayabera shirt he is wearing; he makes no effort to hide it, for to him that would be as silly as trying to hide the shirt itself.

Echenique pauses slightly, then continues to explain, You see, we had vehicles provided by the U.S. government that were light and quick and easy to maneuver, and it was a rout. The *Castristas* had these leftover Stalin tanks from the Second World War that the Russians had Castro. These old tanks were slow and heavy and were sinking in the fine sand of the Cuban beaches. Oh! We were so sure of a win; it would have been a stroll into Havana and an easy defeat of Castro if the unthinkable had not happened, as our worst nightmare came true that day. As the battle increased in intensity, we were running through the munitions like a water hose that has been left on. But through most of the time we were not worried, for we knew that supplies were coming, reinforcement would be there any moment, we could feel it, sensed it in our souls that any moment they would be there, along with the air support, but it never happened. As you know, Kennedy changed his mind, not at the last minute, but well past it. If he had been having those doubts he should of spoken up a day or two before and he would of spared the lives of many men, and the suffering of so many, along with their families. This was perhaps the most ironic point in my life. So absurd! So unfair!

Echenique pauses to catch his breath. His voice has been filling with emotion as he shares with me this most sacred event of his history, one of his Cuba's darkest events. His face floods with the recurring waves of these emotions. The pain of this experience is so evident on him, I feel as if I could touch it. He continues speaking, making no effort to hide his feelings. "We were but moments away from winning this battle and on to an almost assured victory, and it was taken from our hands as we touched it. The scene on that beach, on the battlefield, was one that I will never forget. Grown men standing around with what was an impressive amount of armaments for that era, but with no ammunition for it. It was all so useless. Men standing around, crying out of frustration, out of a lack of understanding that the promised support never came."

Echenique's voice and the cadence of his speech drop, echoing the deep sorrow in his heart. The sadness that he carries with him for those men and that day is still monumental, over four decades later. When asked if he wishes to continue our conversation some other time, to take a break, out of respect for his emotions and level of stress, he declines emphatically: "No, *chico*, how am I to deny you of what you need to know? It is for me a great pleasure to share all of this with you, with the Cuban youth that you are and represent, so that you may prepare yourselves for the future, to carry the cause further until freedom and liberty returns to Cuba."

Echenique continues speaking, further revealing the misery of being captured, of seeing friends taken to *el paredón*, where these brave men were summarily and mercilessly executed. No judge, no jury, no justice. One bullet: one death. On that fateful day, on that beautiful Cuban beach of Girón, with its glistening white sands lined with royal palm trees and turquoise waters, embraced by warm, soothing winds, lives were changed, lives were ended. Families lost their sons, fathers, husbands and brothers, to death delivered by the bloodstained, merciless hands of Castro's soldiers.

As one of the higher ranking politicos on that scene, Echenique's life was spared, but he survived that day at a price: he spent the next two years in the darkest, dampest recesses of the Cuban prison system, a system that makes Alcatraz look like Club Med. After those two miserable years he was able to escape from the prison, and eventually from the island, and he made it back to the United States in 1965.

Echenique has continued to be active within and outside the exile Cuban community. In the mid- and late-1990s Echenique was consulted by Senator Jesse Helms on the Helms-Burton Act. He states that he had forewarned Helms that it was not a good policy or law. At that time he had predicted that the 3rd article (Title III) would not work, would be unenforceable and counterproductive to the anti-Castro cause. "It is like a sheep without wool: there is no production. It implicates any other country that trades with Cuba and attempts to punish them. What it really does is, like the embargo, [give] Castro a further excuse not to pay his debts and an opportunity to further his cause of exposing American imperialism. How can we tell other nations, the British, the European Union, Canada, Mexico, and others, not to trade with what should be an insignificant nation, while the U.S. continues to trade with China so much? There may have been the best of intentions behind the enactment of this law, but it is a utopian pipe dream — it will not succeed. Look how the article (Title III of the Helms-Burton Act) has been suspended every six months by the president. Why? Well, because the United States will always find it to be unenforceable."

I find this an opportune moment to return our conversation toward the subject of the embargo. As the embargo, Echenique's voice continues to betray his emotions. Still he takes no action to hide his pain, his feelings or to place any spin on his words, his truth. I am greatly humbled and honored that this man feels so comfortable with me, so trusting of me, that he can share these events that were so instrumental in forging his life, mind, and soul, without any apparent reservation. Although it is probably partially a result of the long shared history of our families, I can sense that it is also important for him as a member of the "old guard" to pass this information on to me, to hopefully inspire the apparent apathetic attitude of my contemporaries, the first Cuban-American generation, the sons and daughters of the exiled Cubans who have become accustomed to life in this great nation and are nowhere near as involved in Cuban politics as we should be.

When asked if he identifies himself as pro-embargo or anti-embargo he replies quickly, decisively and emphatically,

Neither. I am a Cuban, no more, no less. No other tags or titles need to be attached to that. The embargo is and has been a failure because it was never enforced. The United States selectively enforces or ignores it, as [deemed fit by the administration currently occupying the White House. If the United States and the rest of the world really stuck to it, like what happened in South Africa, then, yes, I would support the embargo, as I did in the beginning and for many subsequent years. But how the American government manipulates it, changes it to fit their current mode, [makes it] worthless and actually hurts those that it [is] said to help. *This is politics, not truth.* I do not like the embargo because it benefits Castro. Although this is not the stated goal of it, Castro has been good at taking it and selling it to his advantage, and Castro does this very well. Castro *needs* the embargo, it provides him with an excuse for his failed economic policies, and so he must have it. Why do you think that every time there is talk in the U.S. government and reported in the media about weakening or undoing the embargo, that "something" always happens that makes Castro look bad? He plans these things. Do you think that the Cuban air force would shoot down unarmed Cessna planes being flown over international waters by the heroic men of Brothers to the Rescue without Castro being well aware of what was going on? What is more, as such a controlling dictator that he is, it would be naive to think that Castro did not actually order those planes to fire…. Look at the timing of these and other similar events. What was happening in the United States at the time? There was a great debate on Capitol Hill as to the necessity of the then-proposed Helms-Burton Act. It was slowly being dismantled into a very light and ineffective political statement. Most of the sanctions were being chipped away, and all the teeth in it had already been removed. After the downing of the planes in 1996, there was a huge uproar, Castro was repainted as a tyrant, his head was called for on a platter, and that platter was deemed to be the now "improved" Helms-Burton Act. All of the strong language and provisions that had been previously removed were quickly re-inserted and it was rapidly passed by Congress and signed into law by then President Bill Clinton. *That* was what Castro wanted. He didn't want a weakening of the embargo. As I said before, he needs it and those actions he took or ordered insured that for the time being the embargo would remain in place.

As our conversation progresses, Echenique's voice rises as he provides this analysis. Like a typical Cuban he is speaking his truth with his heart, does not tiptoe around the subject, and is emphatic, punctuating what he believes to be important, with the conviction of a man who has sacrificed plenty for a very worthy cause: the salvation of his country from a tyrant. Yet Echenique remains pleasant, frequently stopping to make sure that I am following his arguments, that I understand the logic behind them, much like an effective tour guide on a open-sided trolley endeavors to make sure that tourists not only see sites, but reach understanding as to why they are there, why sites are important enough to be considered attractions, and how all these sites are related.

By this stage of our discussion, I am hooked, completely immersed in the sea of Echenique's reasoning and convictions. I am as drenched with his imparted knowledge and experiences as the magnificent, colorful and dynamic coastal coral reefs of the Cuban beaches are drenched by the ocean. I pause briefly to further savor and reflect on these gifts Echenique has provided to me, just as the reefs emerge with the low tides, and appear to survey and reflect on the vastness of the waters around them.

For Echenique there is no pause, no moment to reflect; he has an ever present sense of urgency. "Castro does appear to need the embargo, and the United States will continue to manipulate it as dictated by its political needs. Castro is not only well aware that there is a flourishing black market that has been in place for decades, but he allows it to continue in place. This is an area where he has allowed a thin sliver of capitalistic light to enter the dark communistic failure of the Cuban economy; without this black market, the suffering of the people would be too great, and the ensuing civil unrest could possibly be too much to contain."

Echenique is animated as we discuss the recent economic and political events of Cuba. Once again his voice rises as he speaks of the latest round of incarceration, trial and sentencing of Cuban dissidents, or the latest trade restriction imposed by the United States, or the irony of the recent trade deals made between Cuba and the US. His face fluctuates from soft and serene to hard and set, with stops at all the emotional points in between. Despite this, his voice remains smooth, his gaze firm, providing support to his ideas, ideas that tend to be well thought out, simplistic at times, but convincing.

The United States may be guilty of capitalist imperialism, and it is against this that Fidel Castro has rallied the Cuban troops and to some extent the population, but it is ironic that from the beginning of his regime he has participated fully in another type of imperialism: the attempted globalization of communism through whatever means possible. Further, Castro pursued this agenda to such an extent that it led to the demise of his greatest benefactor, the Soviet Union. Echenique agrees with me on these thoughts and then expands the argument:

> Fidel Castro used the Russians. They were the highest bidders, so he aligned himself with them, although his ideology when he took power was more in tune with the Chinese. As thanks to the billions of dollars that the Russians gave to shore up the failed Cuban economy, Castro facilitated leading the former superpower into bankruptcy. The expansion of the USSR into Africa, South America, the Caribbean nations, and Central America was done at the persistence and suggestions of Castro. The Soviet Union was a nation of peasants, a society that includes an impressive arsenal of nuclear weapons. These Russians were masters at copying technology, not at initiating [it]. It was not until the end of the Second World War that the Russians had Jeeps. These were initially American-made that they had acquired, eventually copying and producing their own. They did the same with their trucks. The Russians were successful against past invaders due to their awesome military not-so-secret weapon: General Winter. It was that harshest of all seasons that bogged down and defeated invaders, including the Germans. But these armaments that worked fairly well in Russia were a failure in the tropics. As we saw during our failed invasion, our five light tanks that we had on the Bay of Pigs beaches were light but quick, and we were able to quickly outmaneuver those heavy Soviet vehicles and tanks with great ease. Once again, as I said before, if the promised supplies had been delivered, even without the air support, there would be in Cuba a very different country today. As Echenique touches on this subject again, his voice once more betrays the pain and anguish he still carries. Yet, he remains frank on this subject, as with most any other theme I care to present.

Echenique appears to be a timeless man. He is at once here in the present, off to the future, and immersed in the past. It is difficult to distinguish between the person that Echenique was and the person he is today, because despite all the changes through the years, from university student to construction worker to civil servant, nothing has changed within him. The views and ideals he represents and espouses are as firmly rooted today as they were over forty years ago. The conviction in his beliefs are unfaltering, unwavering, and yet he is willing to listen to dissenting views and opinions, much unlike other contemporary leaders. He welcomes a good thought-out argument, and the opportunity to debate in a well-mannered and civilized way.

The only change that I have noted in him over the years is an increasing sense of urgency, a feeling that the fight needs to be passed on to those with less years than he, but that these people, these new fighters for Cuba and her freedom become increasingly scarce with the passing of the years. Echenique and the other wonderful individuals profiled within these pages, and even those I interviewed but was unable to include here, have convinced me, have imparted upon me their sense of urgency, their call to arms for our generation, Cuban or not. There is a great need to stop and listen to our elders, listen to our living history, so that we can take charge and bring about the change needed to facilitate a peaceful transition to democracy in Cuba.

IV

MJ

On the campus of the university near where I live, in a scene repeated on countless other college campuses in the country every summer, young people, still in their early teens and most still attending high school, arrive to experience a snippet of university life. These chaperoned gaggles of aspiring writers, scientists, historians, and intellectual explorers participate in programs of academics and the arts. Here, in particular, a group of ballet dancers from the Atlanta area converge on these cool mountains every summer, to practice their art and escape the oppressive, suffocating heat of the city.

Their graceful forms adorn our campus and surrounding area, usually in groups of four or five. Mostly young girls, they appear to be between ten and sixteen, and they move with suave, silky steps, gliding effortlessly, as on an invincible layer of ice, delicate yet strong. Standing in line at the local Subway or mini-mart, they are up on their toes most of the time, almost as if fearing a spontaneous audition will be forced upon them, or that they will perhaps lessen their craft if seen walking on plantar surfaces. I do not know much about these dancers, how they attained the right to participate in a program at Western Carolina University, but I am sure that skill and ability played a large part in their selection.

Dancers' feet are a crucial component of their craft. All the talent in the world cannot overcome poor podiatric health. As a house depends on a good foundation, so to do these athletic artisans depend on their feet as they practice, again and again, the feats of their trade, attempting to defy gravity, to push their bodies to limits previously unattained, through pirouettes, leaps, and other graceful maneuvers.

Many people were interviewed for this book. The majority answered a brief questionnaire. A few provided a flash of insight as to how the embargo has affected their lives. Overall the common theme is one of hardship and sacrifice by themselves and their families. Some of their relatives died as a result of Castro's policies. Most Cubans, exiled or not, are directly affected by the embargo. Some are very cognizant of it; others either choose to ignore it, have become Americanized, or simply don't care anymore. But the fact remains that the embargo, a failed policy of the United States, impacts the lives of many on a daily basis.

One glimpse afforded me was of a person who only identified herself by the initials MJ. Asked how the embargo affected her, a Cuban exile in the 1960s, she replied: "Like everyone else in Cuba ... my feet are deformed, due to their growth at that time in my life and the inability to find shoes. So, as my size increased, my parents had to cut open the only pair I had, causing the irreversible damage."

For MJ, the lack of properly fitted shoes changed not just her feet, but her life and aspirations. As a young girl, her dream was to be a ballet dancer. But in the 1960s, Cuba, in a manner similar to the United States during the Great Depression, found itself without goods typically taken for granted in most countries. The embargo created the opportunity for Fidel Castro to increase control on the Cuban people by limiting stocks in stores, including supplies of clothes and shoes. Castro then imposed more controls on the population, creating food and gas ration cards, and nationalizing stores. Parents throughout the island faced great challenges. They searched and labored extensively to provide what was needed to survive, food and basic clothing. For most, regular shoes were a luxury item, and ballet shoes desired by a young girl were an impossibility. If necessity is the mother of invention, then desperation is the bastard child of austerity. If you cannot provide new shoes to protect the delicate soles of your child's growing feet, then recycling old shoes is an attractive alternative. If the shoes happen to be too small, then cut the tips off. MJ's parents, facing no other alternative, did just that. For MJ, having her shoes cut open to allow her toes to protrude, led to the eventual harsh reality of feet becoming so deformed that by the time she arrived in the US as a teenager, walking was painful, and running or dancing close to impossible. Many times for her, even walking was a personal duel of willpower versus pain. To this day, MJ states, every time she gets up in the morning she is reminded of Fidel Castro and the embargo, as she puts on her shoes. Her hammertoes painfully remind her of those events of her youth.

MJ

Eventually the embargo would ensure that her parents could not afford to buy those shoes even if they had been available. By the mid 1960s, Castro had implemented a full-fledged control of the population, through many means, including ration cards for all basic items. To buy shoes you had to obtain the "right" to be able to purchase them. Then you had to be able to find shoes, and hope that these were the right size. In a twist of fate for MJ, just prior to leaving Cuba, a friend of the family gave them his right to buy shoes, and her parents were able to find and purchase shoes that fit reasonably well. New shoes. New country. New life. But same old damaged feet.

MJ is older now, with a family of her own. She continues to express regret in not being able to pursue those dreams of becoming a ballerina, and places the blame squarely on Castro and the embargo. With the passage of time, her feet have become more deformed, as if unable to stop the process initiated in her youth, back in Cuba. Buying shoes has become an ordeal, as they must fit just right or the pain makes them a torture device.

"It is hard for me to find anything comfortable, especially now that I am older and heavier. I reshape all shoes, since those hammertoes protrude from the leather, and my feet are horrible looking when I wear sandals." But there the regret ends, for she is very grateful that her parents made the sacrifices that they all had to endure in order to eventually be able to leave Cuba.

Mention of the trip of the late Pope John Paul II to Cuba in early 1998 brought a wave of recollections and emotions flooding back into her thoughts: "I was very touched [with] this trip in particular and personally related to each and every ovation he received as he made his way through Cuba." The televised coverage of the pope allowed her to see parts of Cuba that she had never experienced, letting MJ be there, feeling the crowd, the heat, the adoration, the hope and loss, all rolled into one, as people poured out to receive the word of God, the power of hope, and the hope for power over their own destinies.

Glued to the television set during those days, MJ felt she was there in the flesh. The scenery was for her "icing on the cake." Seeing the pope on television, addressing the adoring crowds in Havana, reminded her once more of all the sacrifices she and her parents had to endure to place her "in the winning circle. I realize how blessed I was to be able to give all honor and glory to God, as often as I wish and as loud as I want to. In fact, this was a reaffirmation that my parents' decision to bring me to this great land was the best decision ever made in their lives."

The embargo brought an isolation of Cubans that Fidel Castro used to his advantage in numerous ways, including expelling as many of the religious as he could from the island. In subsequent decades, most Cubans have been denied access to religion. Bibles became impossible to obtain, frowned upon or even banned outright by Castro, and the embargo denied the opportunity to bring more onto the island.

The scenes on television, of a vast crowd, thirsty for the knowledge of God and Christ, left a lasting impression on MJ and untold others. The pope's visit was an occasion of joy and hope for those Cubans on the island, as well as the exiled community. The parallel with communist Poland and the subsequent liberation of that nation was too strong to ignore. But not only was hope for a returning freedom felt and desired by all, but a sense of awe permeated the spectators in Miami and around the globe, for surely this was the witnessing of a miracle — hundreds of thousands of Cubans, with no prior religious upbringing, spontaneously embracing the Christian word brought to them by the pope.

"As you well know, most of them had never had anyone teach them about His greatness. How someone can live and prosper without God in their heart is incomprehensible, so the chance they got to put Him there through this experience and the Pope's blessings and intercession made this freedom one I will never take for granted again."

For MJ and her family, the embargo led to difficulties, lost dreams, and lost hope, but these were eventually regained, along with freedom, when they fled Cuba. The loss of Cuba and all things associated with the island was a difficult price they had to pay for the opportunity to live and worship freely, without fear of governmental oppression and repercussions. This message was poignantly brought home to her by the pope's visit to Cuba. "I usually tell both my parents that there [was] no greater gift than to have to put themselves last and me first in fleeing our country, even if it meant leaving all things and loved ones behind. It was not easy at all for the three of us to live in exile [in the United States] during the 60s, but this trip to Cuba of the Blessed Father gave me another opportunity to revisit those feelings and to once again realize I came out ahead. Thanks to my parents' sacrifice I have been able to remain in the winners' circle in more than one respect."

MJ

It has been a difficult journey for MJ, a long, arduous path, but she remains grateful to parents willing to sacrifice, willing to instill a faith and love of God strong enough to overcome a lack of shoes and loss of dancing dreams.

V

Elpidio

A clear, firm, male voice answered the phone in Spanish: "*Oigo*" (Listen.) Not a question, nor even a statement but something to let me, the caller, know that whatever I wished to say would be heard and responded to, that he was ready to listen.

"*Buenas noches, el Doctor Elpidio Perez, por favor?*" I had called this Dr. Perez in Miami for an initial interview with him in June 2002. At this moment I thought I had reached a wrong number. This was not the infirm, quavering voice of an 83-year-old man; this must surely be a visitor, maybe his son, or perhaps I dialed wrong. After a couple more queries, I realize that I was pleasantly wrong, for indeed this was Dr. Perez, the person I wished to reach. As we exchanged pleasantries and inquiries as to our health and families, I began to feel the admiration that I have come to feel bathed with whenever I meet or speak with this man.

Elpidio, as he prefers to be addressed by friends and families, has been a close personal friend of my parents since many years before I was born. A Cuban-born lawyer, he was also affectionately called "a walking encyclopedia" by his friends, due to his constant and voracious thirst for knowledge, coupled with ease of providing and sharing his knowledge with anyone who cared to ask. All you had to do was be willing to listen. "*Oigo.*"

As we conducted our interview in Spanish, I could envision him seated at his desk, pen and paper at hand, ready for me. His home is a small, modest apartment carved out of a larger residence in the midst of Little Havana in Miami. This tall, proud man, with thin gray hair, pleasant oval face, and easy smile, shares this impeccably clean home with Berta, his wife of over sixty years. They live simply, own an old Honda that amazingly continues to run, and could easily be mistaken for anyone's grandparents in most any setting.

This is the "Henry Kissinger" of the exiled Cuban community, as he has been called. He is not interested in material wealth; for other than his family, wealth for him is knowledge. Elpidio has dedicated his adult life to battling the injustices of Castro's regime. For this he had to flee the island, arriving in Miami on June 12, 1966. A well-educated man, the son of an educator who wrote textbooks still used in Cuba to teach children to read and write, Elpidio removed his children from the Cuban public schools six years before he was able to leave, due to his dismay caused by the indoctrination and misinformation that was being forced into their young minds. Elpidio's love for knowledge and books is such that at great personal risk he smuggled out of Cuba a full set of the encyclopedia *Espesa*, the Spanish equivalent of *Britannica*, just prior to his departure, rather than leave them behind and be destroyed as "counter-revolutionary" material.

As we discuss the embargo and its affect on his life, his voice remains clear and strong. He has studied this subject in detail, and is very informative. Part of his life now revolves around the weekly political newsletter he publishes and cowrites. His replies are intelligent and well thought out, delivered in a rational manner, as you'd expect an intellectual university professor to do, at times peppered with Latin phrases and colloquialisms, but never an obscenity. In response to why he felt he had to leave Cuba, he replies: "*Vis compulsiva*." He "needed to."

Elpidio's voice briefly betrays him, as he further explains why he did not remain in Cuba, having fled while leaving his elderly parents. "My daughter was in Catholic school at the time; my son I was teaching him at home. So they [government authorities] decided to go after her. They started coming to the school at all hours, closing the school saying there was a bomb threat. This went on for a while, then they started saying that my daughter was involved in the bomb threats. All along they were squeezing me, making other false accusations against me, building a case, but had not yet detained me, because I had always vocalized a nonviolent protest and resistance against the regime. I think they respected that, up to a certain point. But once they started to build their "case" against my daughter, I had to leave. That was when I was squeezed too hard. I left my poor parents behind. My dad died and was buried there, and at that point, 1973, my mom was left alone. They let her come here in 1974. I am glad I was able to see her again before she died later that same year." This will be the most somber moment in our interview, Elpidio's voice low, hinting at the great sorrow lurking beneath his words.

When asked to describe himself as pro- or anti-embargo, he firmly replies: "I fight Castro." He proceeds to explain that for him the embargo is a U.S. political tool, no more, no less. Cubans need to fight Castro with whatever means available to them, but the embargo is a U.S. problem, not a Cuban problem. "The solution to the Cuban problem of Fidel will have to come from us, the Cubans, exiled or not. For us to think that the U.S. or any other nation is going to solve our problem is a big mistake, one that I fight against constantly." He describes how every election year, "presidents and other political hopefuls come to Miami, to Calle Ocho, drink Cuban coffee, give speeches, maybe even play a little dominoes. And they all do the same, they say 'Viva Cuba Libre!' so we give them our support, they are elected, and we don't see them or hear those words again for another four years." He easily accepts this as part of the way of political life in the US, something that reinforces his belief that change in Cuba will come only from Cubans. There is no anger in his voice, no resentment. This is just one more fact in the professor's lecture, the way it is.

During a subsequent visit and interview with Elpidio at his home, he explains,

> Eisenhower established the embargo for political reasons in 1960. This was an executive decision; one done without the American Congress, although eventually in 1996 Congress formalized the embargo through the Helms-Burton Act. The Cuban revolutionary government was less than two years old at that time when relationships were severed. Initially sanctions were imposed in an effort to [get] Fidel Castro to agree with requests by the United States government. The acts committed by Fidel Castro against American interests in Cuba were further aggravated by this being in the midst of the Cold War between the United States and the then Soviet Union, a formidable adversary that was strategically poised to gain control of Cuba. Or so they thought. Castro is smart, was astute in the manner he played the Soviets, although it was at some cost to him. As Castro was obligated to cease commerce with the United States, he had to turn and depend on the Soviets. This was most evident in the sugar industry, where without the American technology he had to submit to the substandard Soviet hardware and equipment. Even then, he never did capitulate one hundred percent to the Soviets. As the embargo limited Castro's options, he sought ways to circumvent it while attaining a certain independence from the Soviet Union.

Elpidio pauses, his voice still strong, and offers some Cuban coffee, which his wife quickly prepares and serves before a chance to decline is tended. He frequently pauses to patiently make sure I am following his train of thought and reasoning.

"With the embargo in place, the Soviets thought they would be able to take advantage of it to control Cuba. But Castro managed to stay ahead of them, and in 1964 placed the entire communist party on trial, through the trial of one man, of Mario Rodriguez, a minor individual associated with the communist party in Cuba, that was controlled by the Soviets. Through this means it became obvious that Castro was willing to establish a Castro communism, not just communism. The Soviets realized that Cuba was a great prize for them, so in the end they put up with a lot from Castro."

"So, although the embargo caused Castro to have to purchase the inferior Soviet products rather than the American ones he desired, Castro also realized that having the embargo in place would allow him to further tighten his controlling grip on the Cuban populace. One means of doing this was by establishing the *Comite de la Revolución* (Committee of the Revolution) and [using] it as a means to suppress human rights and stay in power."

As we sip the potent coffee offered in diminutive cups, as is customary, Elpidio proceeds to discourse on the rights trampled in Cuba subsequent to the implementation of the embargo: "These were rights taken for granted in democratic countries: the right to communicate, the right to assemble, to live where you wish to live, the right to decide for yourself; these and others were suppressed by Castro. This would never happen in a country such as the United States, for there is legislation guaranteeing rights and giving recourse against abuses by the government. As an individual you have acquired rights ... but human rights are those rights recognized as a part of humanity, of being a human, a more precise and precious right that has been incorporated recently into the constitutions of most modern countries. For Fidel Castro the embargo was the best thing that could have happened to him. It insured that he would remain in power and maintain his [regime]."

Elpidio and I discuss how, regardless of whatever Castro's form of government is titled, an imposed socialist system depends heavily on the established power of the existing government. And as Elpidio states, in Cuba, "Castro is the government. He has structured it to control the Cuban people. Castro is the great giver and the great taker, from the most elementary detail on up."

In March 1962, while Elpidio was still living in Cuba, hoping against all indicators that his beloved Cuba would be able to right its course and remove the threat to the nation of Castro, Castro imposed the ration card. For Elpidio, that the ration cards came as an alleged result of the embargo is a point he wishes to emphasize: *"Anote, que esto es importante joven."* (Make a note of this young man, for it is important.) "The ration card was imposed as a further method — another tool to control the people. It was not needed as a result of the embargo, as Castro claimed, but was imposed as a means to further control Cubans in a more efficient manner, while suppressing more of their rights, their rights to acquire food and goods. Castro [convinced] Cubans that the ration cards were needed, as the Americans had imposed an embargo and goods were scarce."

The recollection of these injustices causes Elpidio's face to become flushed with anger and sadness. For him the manipulation of the embargo by Castro, for the sole purpose of controlling the Cuban people and stripping them of their human rights, was an evil act, a travesty.

"It is amazing that so many nations, the United States, Canada, European states, and others that profess to be stalwart defenders of human rights, can sit idly and watch the abuses committed in Cuba without so much as a peep." This is said almost as a whisper, a rare moment when Elpidio briefly shows weariness.

Elpidio was surprised initially when Castro opted for the dollarization of Cuba's economy. "Fidel Castro must have done this for financial reasons, not economic. Yet how can a country claim to be a sovereign state when it does not own its own currency? Elpidio launches into a lengthy lesson on how the G-7 nations, initially G-5 following World War II, moved to have currencies' value declared by fiat and tied into the GNP of each nation. Elpidio asks that "Who can establish a value of Cuba's pesos if it is using the currency of another country and Castro will not divulge Cuba's actual GNP? Castro can continue to claim economic hardships, apply for international monetary assistance, all the while not divulging the true extent of his disastrous fiscal policies." This is seen by Elpidio as another means to control the country further while continuing to use the embargo as an excuse. "Castro benefits well from the embargo. He works hard to put a farcical front to denounce the embargo, all the while making sure not to push that envelope so far that the embargo is actually dis-mantled. The embargo serves as an excuse for Castro to hide behind and justify in certain ways that the responsibility is not his for the difficulties suffered by the people."

"This advantage allows him to oppress and control the people while entrenching him in power for 47 years, as of December 31, 2006. Castro uses the embargo as he controls. He does not allow people to see and visit with each other, to deal in commerce, or to have access to real informa-tion. There is no access to books, no books in circulation, no exchange of ideas, and no true knowledge of what is happening in the world."

I ask Elpidio if the dissidents in Cuba are perhaps a small counter-measure to this. He does not think that they are truly effective at any level, for "their libraries are like a grain of rice in a sack full of rice; such little information is lost in the vast expanse of misinformation and no informa-tion."

"The Cuban system is a closed society ... needed by Castro to be able to control. It is a system established expressly for centralized power, and it needs the embargo to provide the rest of the world, the *come bolas* (fools), the so-called intellectuals, that believe Castro is the victim, and see the embargo as proof of that victimization. The day the embargo ends ..." Elpidio's voice trails off, but the gleam in his eyes says it all. I hope he will still be here on this earth the day the embargo is gone, and will be able to see the faces of Castro's supporters and the embargo's supporters as they realize that they have been had, one and all, by Castro and by the United States and its embargo.

The belief that the United States is pursuing its own objectives while stating an altruistic goal of helping the Cuban people with the embargo is evident once more. "Why does the United States not mount a campaign to inform the Cuban people about the embargo and how to change it?" Elpidio asks rhetorically, and answers, "Because it is for the advantage of the United States to keep this embargo in place and pretend that it is doing something, when in actuality it is doing nothing. Fidel Castro in power helps balance power in the Caribbean basin, and that appears to be a desired objective by the United States, a method of dominating the region while protecting other nations from the threat of Castro's communism."

Yet Elpidio also sees this as a two-way venture that also benefits Cas-tro, allowing him to solidify his grip on power. "The Cuban government in 1934 suppressed the Platt Amendment, along with receiving back from the United States all the bases in occupied in Cuba except for Guantánamo. The United States occupying Guantánamo is good for Castro as it provides an alternative means of communication with the U.S., and can also serve as a method to create further conflict as needed."

This is but one of several agreements that Elpidio points to that show that there is a level of cooperation between Castro and the U.S. that tends to be kept under wraps. "Look at how Clinton agreed to return intercepted rafters through Guantánamo. Why? Why did the United States agree to do that? To essentially become the de facto Coast Guard for Cuba? Because it is convenient to United States policies, and the suffering Cubans be damned!"

This is a particular example of the Jekyll and Hyde attitudes that I have also observed of the United States government. I have discussed this with Elpidio and many others, ultimately arriving at the following question: United States officials believe in keeping the embargo intact, are aware of the dismal standard of living for ordinary Cubans, and choose to believe it is a result of the embargo, an embargo placed and enforced by the United States alone, but how does it look to them to have a continued flood of refugees entering the country in a high-risk, high-mortality manner, when the embargo is supposed to help these people.

The conversations I have with Elpidio are always enlightening. We can discuss a wide range of issues, yet we usually end up discussing Cuban politics. Elpidio is as much at ease and in command of his knowledge on other subjects as he is on Cuba. During one of our initial conversations, he asked me to pinpoint where I live, which currently is in western North Carolina, surround by the beautiful blue vistas of the southern Appalachian mountains. He then provided me with an impromptu lecture of this area's social and political history, with great detail and subsequently verified accuracy. Another conversation took place soon after my return from living and working in Alaska over the summer months of 2004. He immediately amazed me with his wealth of knowledge about that region, the natives, the economic factors that have attracted scores of men and women continuously over the decades, from the early gold rush days of the mid-1880s, to the more recent king crab boom of the 1980s, the oil pipeline, and today's events, including the proposed natural gas pipeline, the disastrous policies that the current Bush administration seeks to implement in ANWAR (Arctic National Wildlife Refuge) and the small community of Cuban exiles that have elected to create for themselves a refuge in that wonderfully wild state.

Another more recent conversation touched on the apparent apathy of subsequent generations of Cuban Americans following those who that fled to the US. Elpidio sees the lack of conviction about Cuba by most of these Cuban Americans as a result of assimilation into American society. "These younger Cubans, born and/or raised here in the United States, have become assimilated, and are bicultural, a condition that causes them to be ineffective, much as [hybrid] species, such as a mule, is sterile. This is the result of the exiled Cuban leadership which did not have the vision to predict what would happen and work against it. Instead they came to the United States and became fully immersed in the U.S. political mechanisms, and proceeded to try to apply [one of them] as a means to address Cuba's issues. Bear in mind that this was not the fault of Cubans only, but must be shared with the Americans who also had no clue as to how to deal with the Cuban problem. Therefore, instead of being independent and addressing Fidel Castro as our own problem, we allowed the Unites States to be involved, to take over the process, starting with the Eisenhower administration."

As usual, these conversations center on the embargo and its affects, but meander through a wide range of related topics, causes, and explanations. "The exiled political leaders, [who] had a great amount of experience from back in Cuba, did not realize the need to establish the fight against Fidel Castro independent from any other nation, including the United States. This became most apparent following the Bay of Pigs fiasco in 1961, as subsequent moves by the United States amounted to no more than window dressing, as they had already decided to take a different route on Cuba than that desired by the exiled community. The United States apparently decided to leave Fidel Castro alone, leave the embargo in place and assume a 'wait and see' stance."

Elpidio explains how this relates to the current Cuban-American youth; he believes that the events following the Bay of Pigs led to a leadership vacuum that exists to this day. "With no true leadership in place, all decided to move on with their lives, which led to a stage of adaptation. As exiled Cuban families assimilated into the United States culture, the youth lost that desire to rescue Cuba. This country is geared to assimilate immigrants, not to sustain an exiled community." He points to the Cuban American National Foundation as an example of an institution that is supposed to represent Cubans, yet has become totally submissive to the United States. "How are they supposed to solve the Cuba problem? How can they do this if they are not independent? By assimilation? But not me. No, I am too bullheaded; I am here to work for my country, not to become a United States citizen. Those like me are few, and dispersed like isles in the sea, spaced far apart and difficult to reach one another. We have no consistency in our fight, a fact that is further hampered by the embargo."

I have observed that the current Cuban-American youth, the sons and daughters of exiled Cubans, have become assimilated to the U.S. identity, as is natural to happen. They see how even recently arrived asylum seekers shed immediately their Cuban identity, at times with a disgust so apparent as to be removing a shirt that had been unexpectedly soiled beyond salvation, ripped off the body and thrown in the trash. How can these children raised and even born here be asked to identify with and maintain a Cuban identity when the majority of their parents do not bother to foster that identity within themselves? Parents who do so are rare, and even more rare are those whose children pick up on it and pursue it. I am not talking about going to yell and scream on street corners, and block highways, but a sense of identity from within, a sense of belonging with Cubans, a sense of yearning for what is the true Republic of Cuba, an inner identity that should be natural, so that when asked, "Who are you?," the response is "I am a Cuban born in the U.S.," or "I am a Cuban living in the U.S." This is why there is no true leadership among the generations that came after the initial wave of exiled Cubans. The young leaders who the Cuban exile community are exposed to through the media are pursuing careers in local, Florida, or national politics. These are leaders for the Cuban-American community, not for the exiled Cuban community.

Yes, there are a few that are exceptions to that, but they are few and there is no cohesion, no unity. Some of these look to what is best for their interests here, in Miami, and do so while draped in the Cuban flag. But that is not what Cuba needs. Perhaps it is what Miami or Cuban-Americans need, but it is not what is needed by Cuba. The solution to Cuba's lack of freedom, lack of basic human rights, will ultimately come from Cubans themselves. How can people who do not identify themselves as a Cuban be expected to truly work for that solution.

Elpidio

The transformation and assimilation of Cuban youth into Cuban-Americans has come at the hands of their parents, reinforced by actions of the U.S. government. State and federal standards of education do little to provide Cubans with a complete and thorough knowledge of their history. The United States is the beacon that calls all migrants, or so it used to be. It has been heralded as the great melting pot where all are welcomed with open arms; all are encouraged to "be Americans." Although this melting pot looks more each day like a tossed salad, it does tend to homogenize all who enter. We are encouraged to be proud Americans, to stand up and defend Old Glory. In the recent past the US government has gone to great lengths to Americanize not just immigrants and exiles, but even those whose ancestors were here long before Europeans set foot on the continent. Look at any Native American for proof. The Cherokee nation was divided through a forced separation and deadly march along the Trail of Tears; the Yup'ik of Alaska have only recently regained their native language and customs, through initiatives in schools and villages. Closer to Cubans are Puerto Ricans. Puerto Rico is a colony of the United States, for all intents and purposes. In Puerto Rico the children learn in depth about US history, but stateside children are given a cursory briefing about Puerto Rico, at best. Is this the fate that awaits the Cuban-American community in the United States? Not just to be assimilated, but lost in the vastness of this great country?

The divisiveness of the embargo serves assimilation all too well. How can youths reconnect with their roots when they are prohibited to travel freely to Cuba? Imagine being from a New England state, having moved to Florida, and then not being allowed to return to visit your hometown, your roots. As the years pass and your family grows and establishes itself in Florida, what identity do you think the children will take? That of a Floridian? Or that of a New Englander? How will you teach your children and grandchildren what it meant to be from that area? Are you going to take them to Canada and say, "Well, it is sort of like this, but not really we don't quite speak this way back in [Maine, or Vermont or wherever they are from]?" What are Cubans to do? Take their children to Puerto Rico?

My own parents took me, my brothers and sister to Costa Rica so that we could be immersed in a Hispanic culture, learn the language in depth and keep a sense of our roots. As I have learned more about my Cuban culture over the years, I have come to realize that this was a well-

53

intentioned event, a great adventure, but it taught me as much about Cuba as the Florida-based New Englanders' children would learn about New England if they were to exile themselves in Canada. With the embargo in place, and travel restricted even further in 2004 by the Bush administration, there will be a continued loss of identity for more exiled Cubans and their families. That is a tragedy. Cuba is losing precious resources, in the children of the exiled community.

Elpidio shares how he became weary of organizing and participating in marches and protests, objecting to deportations of this or that person, of an activism that got them nowhere, as it was not an essential part of what is needed to foster change in Cuba. "We have become apathetic; few of us care enough to make the sacrifices needed. We Cubans are great people, even when we speak poorly of our country." Elpidio still retains the hope that there are those in the exile community still willing to take on the fight. He sees the fight as having evolved to "where an individual approach is needed, not great speeches made in the plazas."

Elpidio states his belief that, as a result of the embargo, the Cuban communities have become divided. "Here, the exiles think that the Cubans back on the island are all bad, that they have all sold out to government, and will just argue with no real progress toward reunification achieved. Once more, we have no real leadership, no one willing to lead, to quit speaking and create an independent movement to solve the Cuban problem by Cubans, no one else."

The CANF (Cuban American National Foundation) was founded by Cuban exiles to represent the exiled Cuban community's interests here in the United States and in Cuba. This organization has seen its political influence ebb and flow with the times, but you cannot have two masters. The name says it all: Cuban American. As Elpidio and others have proposed, you cannot represent Cuba while you are looking out for your interest here in the United States. While discussing the CANF at a recent meeting of La Peña, an individual noted that "*se puede jugar con la cadena o con el mono, pero no con los dos.*" ("You can play with the chain or the monkey, but not with both.") Elpidio appears to regard this organization as one that is capable of lobbying Washington effectively, but unfortunately does so to protects its interests here in the United States, with at best a cursory consideration of the Cuban problem of Fidel Castro. My requests for interviews with Jorge Mas Santos, the current head of the foundation, have been ignored.

Elpidio

Elpidio pauses, sighs, and rubs his watery eyes. Suddenly the weight of the world, of his world, a world that is centered around Cuba and all things Cuban, a disappointing world, has emerged again to attempt to crush his spirit. He quickly recovers, as he is aware that I caught a glimpse of the heavy cross he bears. "*Elpidio, estas cansado?* Are you tired? *Paremos por ahora?* Should we stop, for now?," I ask. "No" he replies emphatically, with no room for doubt. "No," he repeats, "we need to talk about this it is important; you need to know these things so you can tell it in your book." "*Gracias, Elpidio, pero*—" But "*No, Chico,*" he cuts me short, before I can offer him a way out, "*No, mijo, siguemos, estoy bien.* Let us continue; I am fine," he insists. "There are those [who] travel to Cuba and are criticized for such. But what do you expect? How are they expected to deny family ties? That is a natural thing to do, so don't get angry with them, but look and see how they can be a part of the solution; they can carry oral messages to Cuba, interact with the people, and start the process of establishing a movement that will incorporate the processes of what is happening in Cuba with what is happening in the exiled community. A unifying process, with strength in numbers. How will this happen? I don't know, but I do know it is possible."

Elpidio proposes within our conversations that the exiled have no true organization, no common goal. "There are many willing to lead there small factions, but none willing to unify and lead the entire community. There is no work being done, we [the exiled community leadership] invent a lot, but we fail to organize, and so we accomplish little. What can we do? *Porque con esa yegua es con la que hay que arar.* (With that mare we are left to plow.) We need to work with what we have, but we need to work!"

Many times Elpidio expresses admiration for his fellow Cubans and for the ingrained Cuban trait that seeks to do well, yet he also sees that as a double-edged sword, because he sees so many exiled Cubans with good intentions but no cohesion.

> We all aspire to a better republic. But we never counted on such a time lapse. Castro is not confronted; it is not done. Not by us, not by others that say they have our best interests at heart, such as the United States. America exercises its influence upon the Cuba problem because it must maintain an interest in Cuban affairs in order to be able to reach the goals it desires. Keep in mind that these are not necessarily the same goals that the Cuban people desire. The American public is sympathetic

toward Cuba — up to a point. Historically there has been a cultural interest by the people, and a strategic interest by the American government. The United States attitude toward Cuba changed once Cuba became independent from Spain. Thomas Jefferson was able to buy Louisiana from the French, Alaska from the Russians, and fought the Mexicans for lands that became part of Texas and New Mexico, but he was also wise enough not to go into Mexico while it was still controlled by the Spaniards.

The United States only became involved in the so-called Spanish-American War once it was seen that the Cubans were defeating the Spaniards. Cuba did not ask for their help, did not invite the Americans. To appease the Spanish government the Americans gave them $100 million dollars when signing the treaty for peace with Spain. But an independent Cuba represented a new set of strategic issues for the American government; oil was becoming more and more important, and a powerful Cuba could dominate the Gulf of Mexico and its oil supplies. So the Americans intervened in the war, as a means to insure that it could control what was to happen in Cuba once the Spaniards were gone. The new Cuban constitution of 1902 was then hobbled with the infamous Platt Amendment.

Today's methods are based on such historic motives and attitudes, but are conveyed in a much more technical manner, as now the world will not allow for one country to colonize another, as we have moved into a global economy. This world emphasis on commerce is what leads to transitions, not a transition of just change, but of controlled change.

The United States endeavors to set up itself to control Cuba, its internal riches and strategic geography. The United States will make sure, is making sure, that when Fidel dies, those that follow will be controlled by the United States. It will seek a transition without violence, without a Cuban civil war, with a semblance of order so that there will be commerce to follow.

The sugar mills in Cuba are in great disrepair, but are not beyond salvage. There are mines for metals in Cuba, as it is well known. There is oil underneath her seas. The United States knows this, for it spent a lot of time and money exploring the Cuban sea beds around Oriente in the 1930s.

We pause briefly to have more Cuban coffee that Elpidio's gracious wife has prepared for us. The rich dark aroma fills the air as the *cafetera* produces its own version of Cuban oil, high caffeine-octane, almost jet fuel quality, that rapidly jump-starts the weariest to face the next round of life. Is this, I wonder to myself, what gives oppressed Cubans on the island fortitude to continue, day after day?

Once more we return to the subject of the embargo, as Elpidio continues: The United States embargo is a commercial embargo. It is a policy of economic restrictions designed to allow the Untied States to do as it pleases, when it pleases, with Cuba. Suppose that we believe for a moment, Fidel, that the Cuban markets are based on free market economies. That is called a *"libre con-curencia."* Suppress that free market with an embargo and you will have results, otherwise there is no use in the embargo. That is what happens in Cuba. All is controlled by Fidel and his gangs; there is no free trade. Free trade in Cuba is a lie and pure fiction. Castro destroyed the Cuban industries all on his own, proof that it did not happen due to the embargo.

Confront him … is what we, Cubans in exile and the world, need to do: confront him peacefully. *Un enfrentamiento.* This is not violence; this is to aspire to awaken the Cuban peoples so that they can challenge the absolutist regime of Fidel Castro. Why? Because we must act now to change the course of events in Cuba, for the regime that follows creates fear in me, for everyone will be trying to control it. The United States, men with their own agendas and interests, all will have their strings attached to pull this way and that for political gains.

The Cuban should not allow such a travesty. We should not allow for others to control our destiny for their political gains. We have to wake up and challenge Castro. We must not wait for others to solve our problems!

Elpidio has been able to maintain a calm demeanor, much like the university professor, yet the depth and breadth of certainty of his convictions erupt with a passion that cannot be reined. For this is his true love, his Cuba, his life we are talking about. Pausing briefly, he drops a notch, and continues,

If we organize, we can do it. We do not need to be a great majority, just an effective minority. For we are a split community, split by the United States with the dollar and materialism. The exile of Cubans is ruining Cubans. We should not waste precious resources and energy attacking or defending the embargo, for that is a U.S. problem. And the United States continues to do what is good for the United States, no more, no less, even if it means allowing Fidel Castro to stay in power for over 45 years. That why we have no true representation in the United States, for the Americans say, "it is my way or no way." The United States does not allow an exiled government to exist on its shores. But let them [exiled Cubans] go to Cuba, to infiltrate, to help, to just be there. Let us, the Cubans, determine what our fate in Cuba shall be.

Discussing travel to Cuba is difficult for Elpidio. The desire to return to his dear land is strong, yet he is painfully aware that with Castro in place it is not possible. His voice changes and becomes charged when asked if he has ever been back to Cuba. "No! Never! I am an enemy of the state; they do not forgive." The words are heavy, as if having been forged in steel, set in concrete and left to harden over 40 years. This is a hard fact for Elpidio, one that he has come to terms with, but does not like. Elpidio is always sure to have me note that these are *his* opinions, with no bias other than a sense of indebtedness to his republic.

Elpidio asks if I knew about "*la cerca piñón*," perhaps? Since I did not, he proceeds to explain, always the professor.

La cerca piñón refers to a spiny bush used to make a fence or barrier in the Cuban countryside, that is used by country folks to facilitate rounding up the pigs. During Christmas season, the Cuban farmers experience a greater demand for pork by butchers and the public in general. Typically this is a time of increased pork consumption, as families celebrate the joyous season with traditions that include the cooking of the traditional Cuban roasted pork. The Cuban farmer will take his trained dogs and go round up his pigs that have been allowed to ... range in the area. The pig is a smart animal and will flee when [sensing] the dogs are coming, but the dogs are trained so that with the guidance of their master [they] will ... herd the pigs toward this fence with its sharp pointed thorns. At that point is when the pig, feeling overwhelmingly trapped, will turn and fight the dogs.

Castro has a been a master of herding the Cuban population toward their *cerca piñón*, yet not quite allowing them to get so close as to turn and fight. He pushes to the extreme, as always using the embargo as an excuse, but never quite lets the population feel those thorns begin to prick their skin.

In a revolution, conspiracy is the final stage, as people tend to talk, purposely or by mistake, which can lead to many complications. There have always been reformists in Cuba, even going back to the time of Spain. But what Castro has done is bring in Leninism in order to break the spirit of the Cuban people.

The exceptions to the embargo are deftly manipulated by Castro to allow a relief from *la cerca piñón* for Cubans. The economy that is based upon monies that exiled Cubans send to their relatives in Cuba surpasses the official economy of Cuba. Castro knows this, and endeavors to keep it going ... since it provides a crucial relief that without which could easily motivate the Cuban populace toward a revolt. Therefore, the embargo in that capacity is of great importance to Castro, as demonstrated by his subversive actions intended to keep it in place. For example, the downing of two unarmed planes of Brothers to the Rescue in international airspace, as the Helms-Burton Act approached ratification votes by the U.S. Senate.

Entonces, it is important for us exiled Cubans to go to Cuba, make contact not only with the folks left behind, but with our roots, our history, our republic. We need to go, not to lecture, and not necessarily to listen, but to reestablish that connection between ourselves. We need to keep our hearts and minds open, to be empathetic to their plight, and to offer ... leadership through our example.

We finish our interview with the usual round of pleasantries and inquiries about our families. Then I ask him one last question, as to how he would use a wish if it were provided to him, with the stipulation that it benefits the Cuban people. He laughs, says that my question is "vague but ambitious," and then answers. "I wish to be able to return to Cuba, to provide intellectual assistance at the first opportunity for a peaceful reunion of all Cubans, exiled or not. This is what I continue to write and publish about, not only for me, but for the rest." I am sure that there are those in the community, including myself, listening. "*Oigo.*"

VI

La Peña

Throughout most of Latin America, open discussions (where they are permitted) are conducted in as civilized a manner as possible by adhering to the rules of a discussion format known as *La Peña*. The name literally means "large rock," but it is a phrase that goes back over 300 years to Spain, when men of letters, poets, and other learned individuals would gather at crossroads and other readily identifiable locations, such as, perhaps, a large rock, to discuss current events while sharing news and information. The principle of *La Peña* has remained practically unchanged throughout the years, continuing to provide a venue for discussions and sharing of thoughts, ideas, and even opposing views. The addition of rules and decorum mandated for this open format discussion are of great use in maintaining a certain level of civility among the participants. These ground rules are proposed and accepted before any discussion takes place. The ground rules are necessary, as Cubans tend to be an emotional, vociferous people, loud to the point of almost being obnoxious. They tend to all speak at once, if allowed to, for Cubans are a passionate people, a population that will wholeheartedly discuss an issue but need the parameters of *La Peña* to police themselves and keep the proceedings from disintegrating into a wrestling match.

One particular Peña is located in a classroom graciously made possible by Miami Dade Community College in the heart of Little Havana. The surrounding area is typical of the Hispanic communities in South Florida, with Cuban coffee shops, fruit and produce markets, mercantile stores, and the aromatic presence of Cuban bakeries, each advertising their products and services in Spanish, along with occasional English advertisements, or even a mixture of both, in what has become known as "Spanglish."

The college's hot concrete courtyard is full of planters filled with flowers around the bases of the towering royal palms. These majestic palms and planters are like inflatable lifesavers, into which tall, proud people have planted their feet, standing ramrod, except for the occasional ruffling of locks of palm fronds in the sub-tropical breeze. The oppressive summer heat of Miami gives way to the welcomed air-conditioned coolness of the classroom. It is your typical college classroom, with rows of gray plastic chairs, a dry-erase blackboard at the head, adorned with a small, utilitarian desk and podium. It is clean, functional, and well-suited for promoting these discussions amongst participants.

The themes of this Peña, held most Sunday mornings, always revolve around Cuba, Cubans, and life both on the island and in exile. The ground rules are well-appreciated by the first-time visitor experiencing this organized chaos, who feels overwhelmed, unsure what is happening, much like a driver who passes a wreck on the interstate, with police and paramedics present: while at first glance the scene appears chaotic, there is still a sense of order, of an outcome that will be the best in the end. Such is the feeling of an uninitiated visitor caught in the midst of a group of Cubans, all talking at once, all verbalizing their opinions with conviction, mindless of whether they are right or wrong. Such are the dynamic forces behind Cubans and within Cubans that keep them going on relentlessly, endlessly, and apparently with tiring. Could it be the infusions of Cuban coffee, initiated almost as soon as babies are weaned from their mothers' breasts that fuels this energy? Setting ground rules is wise — and appreciated, with a sense of relief.

This group consists of mostly men. On average, about 25 attend regularly, yet there are always at least four or five women present. Women are not excluded or discriminated against, but welcomed and appreciated as equals. Anyone can attend, as long as they recognize that the themes will deal with Cuba. The composition of the group is as diverse as the composition of the exiled Cuban community in Miami. Here I have met men in their eighties engaging in intellectual duels with people less than a third of their age. The average person in attendance appears to be in his or her 50s or 60s. Clothing styles ranges from casual to formal, with a smattering of *guayaberas*, the traditional Cuban shirt, always present.

The older men present are polite and courteous, and most of them seem to be well educated and very agile in their intellectual capacity. The founder of this particular *Peña* is an economist who has had to relinquish his leadership position due to personal reasons, leaving two other men in its charge. The elder of this dynamic duo is 86-year-old Dr. Beato. When you first meet him, you are immediately struck by how spry, alert and intelligent he is. Beato continues to work in a semi-retired capacity as a medical doctor, seeing patients and keeping regular office hours. A distinguished man, always well-dressed in a tie and suit, hair neatly combed, he drives himself safely, with ease and confidence, throughout the chaotic traffic of Miami. Beato might easily be mistaken for a man twenty years younger, at first glance. He presents well-thought-out, intelligent and articulate responses and queries to the questions and themes raised, quickly and easily reciting accurate and current statistical data to validate his arguments. Always a gentleman, Beato will never utter a demeaning, belittling or otherwise inappropriate remark to anyone, even those who hold an ideological conviction completely opposite to his. Beato is beloved by all who meet him, work with him, and even by those that oppose his views and ideology. His praises are sung frequently by all of these people, and he accepts them in a simple and modest way, quite similar to the way he lives.

The other half of the duo is Alberto Martinez, an energetic man in his 70s. Like most folks associated with this group, Martinez is also well-informed of current events, a blue-collar man whose university studies of economics were interrupted by the revolution. Deeply tanned from decades of working under the sun, clean-shaven, and neatly combed, he is usually found wearing a traditional *guayabera* shirt, casual, yet elegant and proper. This man has in recent years embarked on yet another career: he is the person to fix problems, people problems, at City Hall in Miami, as a just reward for his great efforts on behalf of the successful political campaign of one of the City of Miami's commissioners, Angel Gonzalez.

Martinez is a likeable, pleasant man, with ardent convictions, yet patient and detailed in explaining them to anyone who wishes to listen. He is also a passionate defender of all things Cuban, including, first, the republic itself.

This particular *Peña* was formed over fifteen years ago in order to promote and foster dialogue between different factions of the exiled Cuban community. It appears successful, as there are well-represented thoughts and opinions from all camps. The one exception is the lack of any *procastrista*; the *anticastrista* ideology is strongly ingrained and the predominant common denominator amongst these folks, entrenched along with a strong desire for freedom in Cuba. Yet they passionately differ in their approach and in their convictions as to how to remove Castro and achieve this freedom.

It is these differences that reinforce the need for the basic rules of *La Peña*. Themes for discussions are proposed at the beginning by anyone, written on the blackboard in the order they are voiced, and are usually all addressed within the allocated time period of three hours. The theme can be anything, as long as the person proposing it is willing to go to the podium and voice his or her thoughts.

As mentioned, Cubans are mostly an emotional people, passionate in all they do and feel, which is amplified in their politics. It is these emotions that worry some, as they may lead not to a reunification of Cuban communities, but to a civil war upon Castro's demise. All of that energy of the Cuban communities at large is felt in this classroom every Sunday morning, emanating from this microcosm of exiled Cubans, as these men and women passionately discuss their themes.

There are rational, intellectual thinkers amongst them, just as there are emotional folks quick to speak, judge, convict, and condemn. Yet arguments, speeches and queries are heard in this room, in sharp contrast to the constant hyperbole that bombards the community through the local Spanish-language radio stations in particular. The Spanish radio camp is well represented here, but they must also listen to and respect the opinions of others, in sharp contrast to the harsh exterior where they usually choose to spout their particular ideology without restraint or consideration for anyone else's opinion.

The need to galvanize all of the *anticastristas* is so apparent. Most are blind to the reality that their tactics seem to only fuel further divide, as they refuse to associate with those that do not toe the line to an ideology identical to theirs. This is voiced by several of the day's speakers as they condemn those who are harsh towards the *dialogeros*. The *dialogeros* are as a group opposed to Fidel Castro and his government, yet hold a belief that a dialogue must be initiated and maintained with the Cuban people on the island, including those in power. Sitting in this classroom, I cannot help but ponder, why is it that as patriotic Cubans we must argue amongst ourselves and dare to condemn those of us with a divergent belief in the pursuit of a free Cuba? Why are they wrong in their wish for peace and liberty in Cuba just because they are taking a different route than the one we have chosen? Does the end not justify the means?

Cuban Exiles on the Trade Embargo

Other topics discussed include how the exiled Cuban community is providing an underground economy that stabilizes Castro's disastrous economic policies. Most exiled Cubans have at least one, if not two or more, relatives back on the island to whom they send money. American dollars are the grease that makes the wheels go round for many countries, including Cuba. Several years ago Fidel Castro allowed the state-run shops to accept U.S. dollars, as the influx of tourists with these dollars was becoming ever more evident, following the collapse of the Soviet Union and the bankrolled subsidy of the Cuban economy. Those Cubans fortunate enough to have relatives in the United States or elsewhere, willing to send any amount of money, found the quality of their life to greatly improve. For some household, this meant the difference between subsisting and surviving day to day. The cumulative effect of these small *envois* represents an amount of upwards of $800 million annually, according to sources such as the Economist.com in an article posted on the Internet in February 2003. Some of the participants at La Peña appear to be genuinely surprised by this news. The consensus of the group is that Fidel Castro is obviously well aware of this underground economy. For it is the group's belief that Fidel Castro controls all on the island; that Fidel Castro knows about all that is happening on the island. No detail of life is beyond his grasp, knowledge or ability to manipulate, for it is this totalitarian control of the Cuban populace that has kept him in power for over four decades.

A portion of the group is distressed that this economic subsidy occurs; yet others agree that there is a great need for it. Helping your family in Cuba has always been a responsibility of those fortunate to have been able to have fled the island, or whose parents fled prior to their birth. This sense of responsibility to help those left behind is so ingrained into the exiled Cuban psyche, is such a defining characteristic of the exiled collective Cuban community, that any attempts to suppress it would be like attempting to suppress your own respiratory drive. No matter how long you hold your breath, eventually your body makes you breathe. Cubans, for all of our faults, are a most generous people, have always been, will always be.

One of the elders of the group suggests that the sending of money to relatives in Cuba can be of advantage to the exiled Cuban community at large by not just helping those immediate family members, but also as a means of seeding the island with frequent and vast "diminutive subversive bombs." *las bombitas subversivas* This gentleman stands slowly, steadies himself with one hand on a desk, and speaks clearly, in a raspy but strong voice that amanates from a deeply tanned face weathered by decades of sun. [With] frequent contact with the islanders ... we can demonstrate to them that there is another world, another way of life, and that the path that Fidel Castro has chosen for them, has made them take, is but one of many, and certainly a path that will lead them to nowhere, eventually."

This statement ignites a heated discussion. How could personal contact of the exiled Cuban community with their friends and relatives left behind lead to change? Some members of the group quickly dismiss this notion as nonsense. They propose that we must force ourselves upon the islanders in such a manner that will "make them see" the errors of their ways. The majority of the group erupts in dissent to this notion that we dictate to the Cubans on the island how, when or where they must act and live, for this is exactly what Castro is doing to them now.

A young man, clean shaven, well-dressed in a casual manner, who opted to not identify himself, timidly raises his hand, patiently waiting to be recognized by today's moderator. "*Si joven*," the elderly but firm voice of Dr. Beato gives permission to speak. In a clear, firm, gentle voice, reminiscent of grade school teachers instructing pupils, he asks: "I just wanted to pose a question, to find out why are we condemning these brave men and women, people that are in Cuba, that are eating *el hueso* (the bone), while we are feasting on *el jamón* (the ham)? What right do we possess? They are there, suffering not only the oppression of the Cuban economy, but further endangering themselves, their families, losing jobs, and perhaps life itself, but because they are proponents of dialogue, of change through peaceful means, we dare to condemn them? Absurd!"

Instantly the room explodes again, as all seek to speak at once. The moderator strains to control the fractious voices all rising at once. The energy in the room increases by what seems like a hundred fold, as all present want to respond. Following this initial stampede of voices, the moderator quickly reins in their questions and statements, and a calm descends upon the participants. But this calm is deceitful, as participants are observed squirming in their seats, some noticeably tense, and just a few truly appear patient.

Eventually the audience seems to reach consensus on at least one item: that the exiled Cuban community does have a right to criticize those on the islands. But that appears to be the extent of unity, for all seem to possess different thoughts and opinions as to how we should criticize and in which direction the efforts should be made. This is where we, the exiled Cuban community, appear to be sinking our own boat.

Whether a person is pro- or anti-embargo, a dialogist, a dissident, an opponent, or any of the titles that Cubans wish to give to an increasingly fractioned community, does not seem to matter, nor does it make sense. The critical threshold should simply be the identification of a person as being anti- or pro-Castro. The exiled community would do well in following the example presented by the dissidents living in Cuba. Whether or not they support the embargo, they mostly present a united front in their quest for political change in Cuba. They do not divide themselves into smaller factions based on their particular version of anti-Castro ideology, but see the big picture, the goal of toppling Castro, and are united behind that goal with a common identity of being pro-Cuba and anti-Castro. Divide and conquer is the adage that holds throughout time and cultures. What is ironic is that the exiled community is doing this to itself, and is being conquered by the lack of progress toward change in Cuba. The exiled community is its own worst enemy — as long as the infighting continues. Once a united stance is taken toward Castro's regime, regardless of the details, success should be at hand.

During these heated debates, most of the more rational voices come from the oldest and youngest participants. Could it be that the old ones have mellowed in their age, while the younger ones were not present or maybe not even born yet when the revolution took place? But this generalization doesn't hold up upon closer inspection, for amongst the youngest men present one Sunday in August 2002 was a past world champion athlete known as "El Tigre" (The Tiger), who holds a kick-boxing title belt in his weight class, and who defected from Cuba less than ten years ago. As a member of a group of athletes who endeavored to accompany and protect older dissidents from oppressive tactics by the state police, he too was labeled a dissident and subsequently suffered from measures that limited his career in Cuba, denied him the opportunity to continue his university studies, and left him jobless. Only with great difficulties was he able to travel abroad to compete. Here is a young man who clearly was denied basic human rights, yet persisted in his quest and eventually was able to travel to Chile to compete in 1992, at which point he defected.

El Tigre, perhaps thirty, was invited to speak at this *Peña*, and, while no less passionate in his beliefs than anyone else present, voiced a more rational approach toward the problem of Cuba. After introducing himself, this soft-spoken, well-chiseled man was able to make a very intelligent and rational presentation:

> We need to support the islanders; we need to assure them that we are going to come with the best of intentions, not to fight with them, not to throw them out in the street, not to be judge, jury and executioner of all real and imagined misdeeds, but to work toward a common goal, a common good, the peaceful transition of Cuba from a "has-been" to, once again, the powerhouse of the Caribbean community. We need to provide support by visiting the island, not to go see *las jinetearás* ["the female jockeys" a colloquial term for prostitutes] at El Malecón, and to party, but to go see family, to let them know that we are all still family, all still part of one community. Not to argue ideological differences, but to show, through example, ... the benefits [of living in a capitalist country]. Imagine the impact of going to Cuba and treating your family or friends to dinner at Marina Hemingway, as I recently did. This is what will plant the seeds of discontent; this is what may ignite the fuse, one person at a time, of a *bombita subversiva*, as previously presented by the distinguished Dr. Beato, that will explode, as happened in the mostly peaceful recent revolutions of Romania and Poland. For how do you think your family members will feel as they realize that they are not able to eat, drink, or even set foot inside this restaurant ... that a meal there can cost as much as a month's wages, and that it is all geared toward the tourists, the foreigners, not the Cubans. And this is but one place of many, possibly hundreds, if not thousands. This is their land, their natural resources being exploited for [benefit] of strangers. These types of visits will set the seeds of discontent, as the realities of the failed economic and social policies of Castro become more apparent. And yet all you did was treat them to dinner, without arguing ideology.

As El Tigre finishes his passionate and heartfelt discourse, and steps away from the podium, the room bursts into applause. While they may not admit it outside this simple classroom on this hot August Sunday morning in Miami, they are all in unison, in agreement, as to the wisdom of his words.

El Tigre's presentation is followed by closing remarks from a wise 80-year-old man, as the allotted time for this Sunday is up. "Remember," he says in a clear, strong voice, "that the Pope John Paul II upon his historic visit to our island told us to be a protagonist of our history and not to be afraid. And with that, ladies and gentlemen, it is time to return this room, so we must go."

The exiting of the room, into the stifling heat of a midday in August, is a lengthy and dynamic process. As they exit the room and mill about the courtyard for another half hour or so, men and women greet each other with warmth and affection, despite disagreeing or even being on opposite sides of the Castro debate. How is it that this acceptance and love for one another comes so easily in one-on-one or small group situations, but is not able to manifest itself in the community at large? This has been one of the largest obstacles faced by the exiled Cuban community, a large source of negative energy that continues to this day, more than 45 years after the revolution, thwarting these peace-loving people in their quest for liberty and justice for their homeland. One of the greatest assets Cubans are blessed with, the ability to love their compatriots, appears to be limited to immediate, intimate situations, and not transferred into the greater political arena without great effort and difficulty. Yet I know this cannot be true, for this is the community I grew up in, of caring, generous people, willing to give whatever they can to help the latest arrival, having once been newly arrived themselves. This is a community that spontaneously rallies around an innocent child found floating in raft, in an effort to save and protect him, an outpouring of community support so strong and un-relentless that it took a subversive operation carried out by the Attorney General of the United States to end it.

I had the good fortune of being able to attend several sessions of *La Peña* from 2002 through 2004. On one occasion, a person I found to be most interesting was in attendance. This man, deeply tanned, with large hands, appeared to be in his late 40s to early 50s. I assumed him to be a laborer. But these were the hands of an artisan, a sculptor haunted by a past, a past that is worn on his face for the world to see. As this particular *Peña* was launched, on a cool and breezy Sunday in November 2003, he stood to the side of the room, hands in perpetual motion, deep brown eyes full of sorrow, full of pain to depths I had never seen. He had brought in a mask he had recently created from parts of a palm tree: fronds, nuts, and bark. To him this creation represented the devil of Fidel Castro; the eyes, fashioned of nuts, were almost human, and represented, he explained, the lost souls Castro had killed throughout the decades. The overall effect suggested Fidel Castro, if you employed a small dose of imagination. All present readily agreed with him, once the mask was presented and explained. It was then hung on the front wall of the classroom to serve as a constant reminder of the one responsible for the events leading to our gathering on this day.

I was constantly drawn to this man, his nervousness, his hands, as mentioned before, in perpetual motion, a piece of palm leaf he was holding cut, bent, and manipulated to become a very realistic miniature palm tree by the end of the session.

The discussions of this day centered on recent events, including the Varela project and a dissident known simply by his last name of Paya. Was he a traitor or a hero?

"At least Paya is doing something without waiting for Fidel Castro's death," a woman put forth.

"There is not a democratic atmosphere in Cuba for free speech; he does so at great personal risk," added Dr. Beato.

"*El es un traidor, vendido*" (He is a traitor, a sellout), added another man. From here the debate continued; Paya's perceived merits (or lack of them) were discussed, as was the Varela Project and similar ones, like the Maceo Project. The debate eventually reached the topic of whether or not to grant amnesty to current Cuban officials, once freedom comes to Cuba.

At this point Beato requested and was granted the opportunity to speak, and he ambled slowly to the podium, apparently deep in thought, as he prepared his remarks.

"What we need is a national Cuban dialogue. A project like Varela, by the exiled community, in the exiled community, has no impact in Cuba. Fidel Castro will never cede his power, his control. This is known by all the Cubans in Cuba, as also the rest of the world. We cannot discuss the branches and twigs of the tree while ignoring the trunk. We cannot spend time and effort discussing amnesty when freedom has not arrived in Cuba. The Varela Project can be transformed and adjusted as needed, once it comes into being, but it needs to arrive to that point. *Caballeros*, remember that this project includes *all* Cubans, those in Cuba, and ... those abroad. Look at what it is trying to accomplish, the return of sovereignty to Cuba, a sovereignty destroyed by the communist government of Fidel Castro along with the Communist Party. Our enemy is not the Varela Project, which seeks the resignation of the entire Cuban government, including Fidel Castro and Raul Castro. Once more, there is no need to wait for the death of Fidel Castro."

The men and women assembled on this day took his words seriously and with a lot of consideration. It was obvious to even the most casual of observers that Dr. Beato was a man held in the highest esteem by most, if not all, of the participants present. Even those who did not agree with him took his words seriously.

Topics proposed and written on the board at the beginning of the meeting were brought up and discussed. Mundane items, such as where to park to avoid the ever-vigilant tow truck operator and his fees, were discussed and agreed upon.

A late-arriving participant asked the artist about his mask. "Look at the eyes," says Sergio, the artist, "look and you see the faces of those who have suffered and died at his hand. Men and women and children have suffered because of Fidel Castro. Children? Children you ask? Yes, children also." Sergio was becoming more animated, his face a rapid succession of expressions that conveyed pain and sorrow in one hundred different ways, at times seemingly all at once. His hands flew, like swallows attached to his arms; his body rocked back and forth; he seemed capable of exploding into tears at any moment. "I was 14 years of age when Castro sent me to his prison. I was sent not for doing something, not for being a criminal, but for thinking of wanting to do something. I was sent because my thoughts showed them that I was a 'traitor of the revolution,' for wanting to leave, for my having desires of freedom." Sergio was pained by his recollections, but continued to share his experience with us, attentive to his every word,

> I wanted to be able to have freedom like others in the world. I am grateful [for] being able to come to the United States where my sons are raised free. But I suffer for those that are still in Cuba, still in those prisons I left; they have been forgotten by the world. Because of Fidel Castro and his gang, they are dying in the prisons, dying out [at] sea. Forgotten [and] ignored, sequestered by Castro, the embargo, bad policies of world governments. When I saw on television the atrocities of 9/11, the Twin Towers burning and those above leaping off the burning buildings, only to be torn to pieces upon impact, leaping to certain death, but leaping to escape, I felt for them, and I also thought of our Cuban brothers and sisters, the rafters, launching themselves to sea. But for these Cubans it is

not the flames of a burning building they flee, but the flames of an oppressive regime. And it is not the asphalt that will tear them to pieces, but the sea, the sharks, the drowning. If the world could see films of that on the evening news, Fidel Castro would be gone in two days.

Suddenly, all of Sergio's animation ceases. He spoke at a level barely above a whisper. The entire room was quiet. "*La isla del despido.* The isle of goodbyes. Say goodbye to liberty. Say goodbye to freedom, to your mother, to your family, for it is better to die dismembered at sea than burned to death."

On that day *La Peña* ended a little more somber than usual, the good-byes more muted. Sergio gave me the mask as a present, explaining again in great animation the details and nuances of the features, explaining every bump and fold. I keep it above my desk, and every time I look at it I have visions and thoughts of those of poor souls, victims of 9/11 falling to their death, and wonder how different the outcome of events in Cuba may be if, as Sergio stated, images of the Cuban victims were available for the world to see.

La Peña is a grain of sand of patience and understanding on the beach of Cuban emotions. This beach is made up of untold millions of these grains, each of them as important as the next, for without them there would be no beach, no collective consciousness, no emotions and no sense of country. As the waves of the sea deposit more grains on the beach, build her up to withstand the next tropical storm, so does *La Peña*, slowly but surely promote a rational dialogue and discourse, so that Cubans may be able to survive the civil storm that will most certainly follow the demise of Castro. This group, along with numerous others throughout the exiled Cuban community can be the key to the future of a post-Castro Cuba. As Cubans participate in these groups, participate in the civilized give and take of ideas, and take some of these thoughts and ideas back to their homes and communities, a common ground will be created, I hope, a venue to direct the energy of Cubans, minimize the infighting and bring the needed changes to Cuba.

Sitting in *La Peña*, listening to several of the more divisive speakers attempt to intimidate other participants through a heavyhanded approach that condemned those who did not support a similar ideology, I was once more left with a sense that if we could just concentrate on obtaining our common goal, the defeat of Fidel Castro, if we could unify our efforts to obtain that goal without this incredible expenditure of all this negative energy, then surely we would succeed. But, until the day that these dreams come true, until the day that we present a fluid yet unified front, until the day that we realize strength through numbers, unity through a common cause — until that blessed day we will continue to be our own worst enemy.

VII

Dr. Beato

In the city of Coral Gables, Florida, an oasis of impeccably mani-cured, landscaped homes and streets adjacent to Miami, lives Dr. Virgilio Beato. Dr. Beato lives in a modest two-story Mediterranean style home, with a neatly kept yard and an immaculately clean interior, perhaps as a result of the exacting hospital environmental standards that he is accus-tomed to. Beato is 86 and continues to practice internal medicine, keep-ing regular office hours. Well-groomed, clean-shaven and always smartly dressed, he exudes self-confidence, intelligence and compassion.

Dr. Beato was head of the school of medicine in Cuba, a position for which he is remembered today by legions of Cuban doctors whom he trained before leaving the island nation.

As mentioned previously, Beato is very involved in the political arena of the exiled Cuban community of Miami. His is one of the few voices of moderation, of promoting dialogue and of establishing a rational and intel-lectual approach to the problem of Castro and what will happen in Cuba once Castro is gone from power. As a means of attaining his envisioned goal of bringing together into some sort of cohesiveness the different *anti-castrista* factions of the exiled community, Beato co-directs *La Peña*, a dis-cussion forum that meets regularly on the campus of Miami-Dade Community College. It is at *La Peña* that I first met this distinguished gentleman, and there I was quickly impressed by the depth and breadth of his knowledge, passion and charisma. Dr. Beato enjoys such a high rep-utation, that even those on the opposite side of the *anticastrista* spectrum treat him with respect, dignity and deference.

In a modest Cuban restaurant on Miami's *Calle Ocho*, a large group of exiled Cuban men and women meet to have breakfast. The waiter efficiently escorts the arriving members to a long, well-lit room at the rear of the restaurant, away from the main dining room which is almost filled to capacity at this mid-morning hour, with frantic, almost fanatical energy emanating from patrons and staff alike. Conversations in Spanish abound, rapid-fire and unending. The first impression that greets me at the door of the room is an overwhelming feeling that everyone is speaking at once. I seek a route to my seat at today's meeting in the reserved room at the rear of the establishment, pausing as I follow the leading staff member, to once again evaluate the room, to realize that everyone present *is* speaking at once, some carrying on more than two or three conversations at once. I am grateful to reach my destination, the back meeting room, with its comparative quietness and tranquility. The stucco white walls are sparsely decorated with posters depicting scenic images of Cuba, interspersed with the occasional portrait of Cuba's founding fathers and historic figures: Maceo, Marti, and others, honored in simple frames, left to be visually enjoyed by the restaurant's patrons along with a copy of the Seal of Cuba, occupying a fading gold frame, kept clean and dust-free, despite its age.

The group meeting this morning for breakfast and companionship is composed mostly of regulars from *La Pena* along with their guests. The idea is to meet on occasion in a less formal setting, a locale that would allow all to enjoy a change of scenery from the austere classrooms employed for the regular meetings. Additionally, they have opted for this location in a further effort to foster camaraderie and fellowship amongst all, while beckoning newcomers in a less intimidating location and manner.

As participants and guests arrive, discussions are launched and deepen while a breakfast of scrambled eggs, toast and *café con leche* (Cuban coffee with milk) is served and consumed. In a manner not unlike the main dining room, everyone appears to speak, listen and eat at once, yet the trends of the conversations are much easier to follow. The din and hum of energy flows throughout the room until Dr. Beato takes the podium. Then voices fall and attention shifts completely toward him. Once again, I am amazed at the attention this man commands with just his presence. The respect and admiration that the audience holds for Beato seems so tangible, that I start to think I could take a slice of it home to cherish. An act as simple as standing brings the room to silence; all eyes are focused on him as he begins to speak. The topics that Beato speaks about are fascinating, as is his command of them. He lectures in a steadily paced manner on topics varied yet interwoven by how they affect Cuba: John Maynard Keynes, Cuba's 1940 constitution, anti-liberal socialism, neoliberalism, Social Darwinism, and so on. The lecture eventually leads to current events in Cuba, the embargo, communism, and the possibilities of the future.

Dr. Beato reasons that in order to ultimately defeat the communist regime we must all know and understand what communism is. He emphasizes that the communists were in Cuba before Castro, and only came to be the party of power when Fidel Castro decided to align himself with the Soviet Union, as they were essentially the "highest bidders" willing to fund his egomaniacal quest for total power and control. "Castro must not be dismissed as an idiot," Beato says, "for he has been able to maintain an absolute control over Cuba for more than four decades. He has employed a wide range of tactics to maintain and enforce this control, including the manipulation of the embargo for his benefits."

Over a course of almost two hours Beato has his audience reaching for every word, every idea, as a suffocating person reaches for life-sustaining air. Beato has the gift of being able to take complex material and present it to a general audience in a manner easily understood by most. This, I imagine, must be the result of explaining medical issues to countless students, patients and their families over decades of practicing and teaching medicine. The bad news the doctor delivers is that the critically-ill patient is Cuba, a patient with over eleven million family members, suffering from a large malignant ailment named Castro. But the good news is that a holistic medicine will save this patient, a medicine that can be delivered by any of those same eleven million persons, all quite capable of being the catalyst that precipitates the cure.

One morning, following one of the regular meetings, a discussion ensues about authors who have recently published books about Cuba and the embargo. Dr. Beato responded with statistical data to back his arguments, while we were discussing a particular book. A look at the embargo from a decidedly sympathetic view of the Castro regime, this book most praised Castro's actions as salvation for Cuba from a corrupt Batista administration and imperialist American desires, accomplished heroically despite almost overwhelming odds. Despite believing that this book contains no objectivity, as this author is so blinded by his awe of Castro, I feel compelled to ask Dr. Beato about points the author attempts to make relating to health care access and delivery. Beato counters the allegations that medical access was limited almost exclusively to Cuba's larger cities in the pre-Castro era and that access to medical personnel and

treatments were limited to only the few who were rich and well-connected:

> Up to the year of 1958, before Castro came into power, there were 200
> hospital beds for each citizen in the United States, while in Cuba that
> number was 197. Cuba had 13,000 hospitals at the start of the Batista
> government's rule, mostly smaller, rural facilities, and built 3,000 more
> during the time of [his] government. These were indeed larger with more
> comprehensive health care services and facilities made available to all.
> The economy of the island nation of Cuba was firmly established, with
> one ton of sugar per citizen, as with one head of cattle for each person, a
> definitely prosperous nation, at least by its contemporaries' standards."

Beato presents these and other statistics in a manner that attempts to
engage his audience in a dialogue, not as a confrontational or badgering
assault, but as an invitation to join him at his table and share of the fruit
of knowledge, even though you may not agree with him.

The embargo is a policy that Beato enjoys discussing. He is able to
objectively present the events that led to its implementation, without
influencing or leading the listener. "This embargo came initially during
the Eisenhower administration as a result of the initial actions of the Fidel
Castro government taking over the properties of American nationals. As
the years passed and other administrations came into play, the embargo
grew in the scope and severity of its punishing powers as a means to not
only punish Fidel Castro, but to attempt to topple him. As you can see,"
he says, with a little smile lurking in the background, "it has been a grand
success." Beato chuckles at his statement, then pauses briefly before continuing in a more serious tone. "This embargo has been in place for 43
years at an incredible cost, with no gains for anyone, except for perhaps
Fidel Castro himself. The embargo is said to help the people of Cuba by
fostering the removal of Fidel Castro, but in actuality it is entrenching
Castro more every day, while inflicting pain and suffering upon those people it is supposed to be helping. In addition, this embargo is causing a rift
among the Cuban community, not only between the ones on the island
and those exiled, but amongst the exiled Cubans as a group and amongst
the islanders also as a group. This is of grave consequence, since it could
lead into a civil war in Cuba once the regime of Fidel Castro has fallen.
Will it fall? Yes, eventually — but not due to the embargo. What will cause

Castro to go will be old age. Once he dies, his regime will remain in place, intact and in power, as it should be for a matter of time, perhaps as little as a few months. Then those who were previously aligned with him will begin to seek new alliances and the change that we have been expecting for over four decades will finally arrive."

Dr. Beato delivers these facts, ideals and heartfelt opinions in a cadence much as I imagine he used while lecturing his medical students in Cuba over four decades ago. He displays command of the subject, leaving no doubt as to his investment of time and effort, relentlessly studying and analyzing this complex patient, that the political arena of Cuba presents to him. Yet his approach is more holistic, more of a looking at the whole patient than just at the signs and symptoms manifest during the consultation. He has not only studied the past, but has dedicated as much energy to the present and the future of his dearest patient, his beloved Cuba.

"But what happens if we keep this pressure on the islanders during our exile? These threats that the radicals are shouting toward the islanders does nothing more than instill fear and hatred. How can we tell them that we will come and throw them out on the street, take away the shelters that they have had all these years, [regardless] of how they obtained it? It is a basic human need to seek shelter, to have a place to call home. If it happens that the government appropriated these homes and gave it to these folks, then ... we have an argument for the return of our properties. But we still have an obligation that it is done in a fair and just way, without displacing our brothers and sisters that have stayed on the island all these years. Using the radio stations in Miami to try to intimidate the islanders to return these properties without any due process is not the right way of doing it, and all it is accomplishing is that the level of resentment and fear continues to grow. This is what may perhaps lead to civil war in Cuba if we do not take the time to establish a rational dialogue with the islanders."

Beato remains calm and intensely focused as he discusses these aspects of a possible scenario post-Castro. The love and concern that he has for all his compatriots, both here in Miami and in Cuba, is obvious. Like a father who cannot bear to see his child falter and fall while learning to ride a bike or roller skate, like the father of a child found arguing with a peer in a vicious circle of "Oh yeah, says who?" one-upmanship, he tries to try to inject a little rationality, in the hope that this small acorn of tolerance may eventually grow into a mighty oak of rational and just behavior by all Cubans.

Our conversation turns to recent events associated with the embargo. "As you may know, the United States came into Cuba because it was a strategically located island in the Caribbean. At the beginning of the 1900s the United States imposed its will upon the Cuban people by demanding and having what is called the Platt Amendment written into the Cuban constitution, which gave the United Sates the option to unilaterally decide if the current Cuban governmental administration was appropriate for Cuba, and if not, the authorization to remove any governments not to its liking. This mentality of American imperialism is what has fueled Fidel Castro, and is still alive and well in the American political mind. The recently enacted Helms-Burton Act says, among other things, that the United States will bar any government or business organization that does business with Cuba from entering any United States port or doing business in the United States for a period of a minimum of six months. What is curious to note is that since this passed in 1996, every president has had to suspend this portion of it every six months as required by the act itself. Why? Because if this Title III of this act were to be enforced, it would basically isolate the United States from most, if not all, of its trading partners. Canada, Mexico, Great Britain, Spain, the European Union, all of them do a lot of business with Cuba and with the United States. We could not afford, as Americans, to not allow them to participate in our economy, for it would lead to [its] collapse."

One of the more pleasant aspects of being able to listen to Dr. Beato is how, despite his readily evident love and passion for Cuba and her politics, he elegantly and objectively presents his ideas. These are not presented in the typical boisterous Cuban fashion. They are well thought-out and presented just as he would have presented anatomical and physiological material to his medical students. Beato's reputation as a learned fellow is well-established in the minds of *La Peña* participants, with compliments and accolades heaped on him when he presents his material. Beato obviously takes great care and time to make sure that he is well-informed, not only with timely material, but with factual material as well.

We pause briefly, as Dr. Beato graciously inquires as to my needs. Would I like something to drink, perhaps? I decline, as I am captured in the moment of our dialogue. Dr. Beato's gentle demeanor, eloquence, deeply rooted passion, and love of Cuba and Cubans are quench my thirst at times like these. What will happen to us, the sons and daughters of exiled Cubans living in the United States, once these aging men and women are gone? These people are our living history, and, in Dr. Beato's case, our historians. These are the people who take great care to study, to discuss, to keep safe what has happened and what needs to happen. Who among my generation of Cuban Americans will rise to this unspoken challenge our elders present to us, reinforced as their ranks dwindle, taking with them their unanswered questions and unfulfilled dreams?

We continue with our conversation, sitting in his room, with lightly colored walls, decorations and furniture, full of Florida sunshine pouring in through elegant, though security-barred, windows. The only sound heard in this house is the soft, distant hum of the air-conditioning system in its never-ending battle against the sub-tropical heat.

"The embargo was thought to be the catalyst to enable change to come to Cuba. The thought being that if the Cuban people would suffer enough, they would not to tolerate the regime, and therefore a revolution would ensue," explains Dr. Beato. "But they forgot to take into consideration that Castro would manipulate and oppress his people by whatever means possible. In order to be subversive to a regime you need to be able to meet and conspire. But in Cuba, Castro established the *Committee for the Defense of the Revolution*. The sole purpose of this committee was to police the people through the people. Every city block, every neighborhood, has a member whose job is basically to spy and report any findings, real or imagined, to the authorities. If a visitor comes to your house once or twice, [this] may not be an issue. But if a visitor comes more than that, then the interrogation will follow. 'Why did you meet? What did you talk about? Who else met with you?,' and the like. They can, and do, make your life miserable."

The point is succinctly made: how can you foster a counterrevolution when you can't even meet privately one-on-one? In order to be able to conspire against Castro, dissidents or possible dissidents would have to meet, yet this is impossible without risking a jail sentence, as the Committee members are as zealous today as they were in 1961 when the committee was first formed.

Without being able to conspire, to foment a counterrevolution, there is not much the Cubans on the island can do. There are those who are dissidents, those who support dialogue, and those who are reformists. The American media blur the distinction between these labels, calling all of them dissidents. But these distinctions are important, and it is important to remember that a reformist is someone similar to Lech Wałęsa, who sought to bring change to Poland by working within the country's constitution, calling for a referendum, as allowed within that constitution, much as reformists in Cuba are attempting to accomplish through the Varela Project.

These brave men and women, who initially numbered 11,000, do not consider themselves dissidents, as they do not voice an opposition to their government, but instead labor to bring change by using means allowed with the Cuban constitution. Castro opposes their referendum, for he can see the writing on the wall if it were to pass: the demise of his regime and the devaluation of all he believes himself to be. But this does not make them dissidents, just reformists — and very brave ones at that.

Dr. Beato maintains that trying to economically drown the Cuban government is a waste of time, and that Cubans in the U.S. support this embargo because there are no other options available to them. The need to "do something," even if it is to support a failed policy, is so great, so strongly infused in the collective sense of the exiled Cuban community, that to withdraw the embargo would be akin to asking a rafter to release his raft and attempt to cross the Gulf by swimming alone.

"The embargo is a contradictory policy," explains Beato. "Cuba today buys medicine and food for the first time, as allowed by the exception to the embargo written in American law, to the tune of nearly $120 million in 2001 alone. And [these are] not just cash transactions, as we are lead to believe, but are also transactions that are being financed through American banking institutions. This defeats the embargo."

Outside Beato's home, a subtropical breeze blows softly, causing the shadows of massive banyan trees to dance back and forth across windows, and with it the sunlight ebbs and flows in contrast, much like the synchronous weaving of dancers rapt in a tango rhythm, fluid in motion. The changing light enlivens Beato's features, softening the effects of his 80-plus years, enhancing that youthful exuberant look he possesses.

"For the U.S. to unilaterally dismantle the embargo, Castro will have to go. But Castro will not go, for to do so would be to invalidate his life, his cause, and that will never happen. Castro will go when he dies, then perhaps change will come. But this change will not be immediate, but could follow a 'transition phase,' so to speak. What I think will happen is that Raul Castro will assume power over the country, as is written into the communistic constitution, and will enjoy a substantial measure of support for the moment. *Pero, despues del velorio viene la conspiracion.* (After the wake comes the conspiracy.)"

Beato further maintains, "Once Raul Castro assumes power, it will not take long for him to be seen by the younger Cubans as the old man he really is, and with that they will begin to truly conspire for change, despite the difficulties they will face to do so. Once these younger Cubans control the communist party, they will probably change the name, calling themselves something like 'Social Democrats' or the like, in an effort to be able to pursue their change, soften the adverse relationship with the United States, and bring a much-needed end to the embargo."

Dr. Beato continues further along that trail: "Of course, the United States could bring an end to the embargo sooner, but, for that to happen, the president would have to want such change. If there was no Jeh [Jeb Bush, governor of Florida], brother of Bush [President George W. Bush], and the president wanted change, change would happen. But Jeb needs the Cuban-American community for his re-election [November 2002], and so does President Bush need them for his re-election [2004], so they will do anything to appease Cuban Americans, including maintaining the embargo."

Once again, the argument that the embargo is no more and no less than a political tool, used to further American political interests, including those of their politicians, has been presented. The impact of the embargo in terms of Cubans, here in the United States and in Cuba, continues to take a back seat. I ask Beato to expand his thoughts. Will these policies of maintaining an embargo at all cost, for the benefits of Americans, divide Cubans?

Pausing briefly to reflect on the question, brow furrowing briefly, Dr. Beato answers. "Cuba also has a duality: those in favor of the embargo, and those against, even among the dissidents. But ..." And here he pauses for a moment as if to subtly emphasize what is to follow, to verify that I am paying attention, "These dissidents wisely present a unionized, collective effort. By banding together to better conditions within Cuba, they ignore the embargo, since they cannot control it, as only the United States can bring the much-needed change. But here in Miami, we waste time and effort, insulting those that want to try to change the embargo, without stopping to think that there is nothing ..." And here Beato leans forward to emphasize his point. "There is *nothing* we can do that will change the embargo. It is such a sorry waste of efforts. Cubans in the United States have become divided by tactics, and not by principle, as a result of the embargo."

VIII

Teresita

Fidel Castro and his gang, supported by the embargo, caused the splitting of the Cuban people at many levels. A beautiful and prosperous nation, with the promise of a great future of achievements and advancements, was split, as a well-educated minority fled in the first waves to the United States and beyond. A less educated but just as motivated and vibrant blue-collar wave followed. Cuba's brightest fled, followed by those capable bringing the tasks to fruition. How can a nation survive such a drain of its most precious natural resource? Yet Cuba did survive, as many were unable to flee and faced no recourse but to stay and put their talents to use, most with the hope that some day soon the tyranny would end and life would return to the way it was, that it was just a matter of time, if they could just wait it out and survive. To survive, those left behind depended on those who left for help in whatever form possible: medicine, food, cash, clothes, and such. The divisiveness of Castro's regime affects not just the Cuban nation as a whole, but all communities within Cuba and exiled, including families. Some families had no recourse but to send their children off to the US with not much more than a small cardboard suitcase, hope and a prayer. Mothers and fathers did not know when, if ever, they would see their precious children again. Many never did.

These parents sensed the looming doom brought upon Cuba by Castro, aggravated by the embargo and other misguided policies of the United States. In those difficult early days, families were split, as children were blindly sent to the US, at times with a relative or friend to receive them into their homes. Others, such as the well-documented "Pedro Pan" children, were sent to the US with the hope that they would be guided to the relief efforts of Catholic organizations, which would then move them to group homes or private homes that offered to assist them in their hour of need. In this manner Cuban children arrived at locations far-flung from warm, tropical breezes. In addition to Miami and Houston, Cuban children arrived in Chicago, Omaha, New York City, Union City, New Jersey, and elsewhere.

Other families, the majority of those that fled, were divided, as some family members were able or later allowed to leave, while others couldn't or wouldn't. Elderly parents too infirm to travel stayed behind with sons and daughters too afraid to leave them behind, yet all were supportive and encouraging of those fleeing, such as Teresita (last name withheld by request), her sister, their spouses and children. In the initial years following Castro's revolution, phone lines were tapped or made inaccessible, letters censored or simply not delivered, and the divide between family members grew. But the old adage that blood is thicker than water holds true, even when the water is as vast as the sea that surrounds Cuba, as these families maintain a strong love and commitment for each other that neither time, nor distance, nor injustice will ever diminish.

In recent years, Castro has endeavored to capitalize on sentiments between split families and communities, has taxed international phone calls as a way to generate much-needed revenue. The re-establishment of telephone communications has allowed exiles such as Teresita to speak with family members left behind. This need and desire has grown with the years, as fewer family members remain in Cuba, most having died. Teresita is grateful for the opportunity to talk with her family in Cuba on the phone, and occasionally sends "twenty five dollars, or whatever I can, as they need it. I send medicine too, for one of my poor aunts has glaucoma and the medicine is not available for those like her that don't belong [to the Communist Party], and in the dollar stores [government stores where only the U.S. dollar is accepted, cash only] it is much too expensive to purchase this medicine. *Le doy gracias a Dios* (thank God), that I am able to speak with them on a regular basis, for otherwise my family and I would be unable to help them survive."

Teresita, as with the majority of exiled Cubans with family back in Cuba, feels a moral obligation to help those less fortunate, especially relatives. Teresita is a recent widow and has lived in Miami most of her adult life; her husband had been gainfully employed since shortly after their arrival in the late 1960s. Over the years, with hard work and frugal practices, they saw their modest fortunes increase, and they were able to move from a shared house with relatives to their first modest apartment, to eventually the home she now shares with her centenarian mother. Teresita has sent funds to Cuba, to help those less fortunate than herself, as best as she could. Collectively, the exiled Cuban community has sent, by amounts of less than $100 each, an average of more than $800 million each year to Cuba in recent years. These are much-needed dollars, needed not just by the individuals who receive them, but also by the government, into whose coffers these dollars eventually land, to survive the consequences of the disastrous economic policies implemented by Castro and exacerbated by the embargo. The exiled Cuban community, in general staunch and unrelenting supporter of the American embargo, is by itself defeating the embargo with such seemingly insignificant actions as sending $25 to a suffering friend or relative in Cuba. Obviously it is the collective power of such *envíos* (sending) that defeat the purported intents of the embargo, but to strictly enforce the embargo and absolutely deny the sending of these small sums to Cuba would be a greater travesty, as families in need would suffer greatly.

The administration of George W. Bush has proposed limiting or completely halting the sending of money to Cuba by relatives, as a means to further strengthen the embargo, an ironic move by the stewards of the greatest nation, a nation that has proclaimed itself to be the defender of human rights and democracy on the planet, a nation willing to send its youth to farflung foreign lands in order to defend these ideals, a nation willing to employ preemptive strikes against brutal regimes. Unfortunately these actions are not directed toward Cuba. The US is not intent on removing Castro from power, at least not by employing military intervention or other more direct method than a failed 45-year-old embargo. Other than some sugar, a few mines, and tourism, Cuba lacks what the United States desires: vast amounts of oil. There is oil off of Cuba's shore, but apparently not enough to justify an invasion, at this point.

As long as the embargo is in place, Teresita and her family will continue to send money, medicine and whatever goods are allowed. They will pray and hope for the safety and well-being of families and friends in Cuba. Teresita would like to go to Cuba, to see her homeland once more before she follows her husband to their places at God's table, but she is aware that with the embargo in place this will not happen. She is well aware that travel to Cuba can be accomplished, but the effort and expense associated with traveling within the conditions and limitations set by the embargo are too great for her. For now, she will content herself with the sound of the voices of her family and friends on the other end of the phone line. For now, she will continue to send the occasional $25 and medicine. For now, she will continue to pray for a not-too-distant future that includes renewed freedom in Cuba. For now, she will continue to hope.

IX

Travel and Funds

In June 2004, with little fanfare from the White House, the Bush administration commenced to enforce new rules for travel to and from Cuba. The reported dual purpose of these rules, as dolefully announced through media outlets such as the Associated Press, was to "further strangle Castro's communist economy" and "force out" Fidel Castro.

The new changes restricted *envios* (the sending of money), limiting recipients to immediate family: mothers, fathers, and spouses. All others — uncles, aunts, cousins, and such — would have to find their own, more immediate, benefactors. Friends? Out of luck.

For those traveling to Cuba, the amount of carried cash allowed changed from $3000 per traveler to $300. In addition, Cuban exiles wishing to travel to Cuba to visit family, friends and relatives would now be limited to one trip every three years, compared to the previously allowed one trip a year.

Showing typical politician wisdom, the rules are retroactive; therefore, if an exiled Cuban had traveled to Cuba a year ago to visit his ailing mother, that person would now have to wait two years to visit her again. The dedicated son would hope she schedules her death in a well-timed manner, consistent with the new rules, or he will have to miss out on the funeral.

According to the Associated Press, over 115,000 exiled Cubans living in the US visited Cuba last year, as well as more than 50,000 more exiled in other countries. These people typically travel with large amounts of clothes, medicine, toiletries and other necessities packed into suitcases and cardboard boxes. Usually on the return trips to the US these suitcases come back empty, or close to it. Under the new rules these travelers are limited to no more than 44 pounds, less than the combined weight of two average suitcases. If you travel to Alaska for a week of sightseeing and salmon fishing, most airlines allow you to bring back home up to 50 pounds in frozen fish, as well as your other suitcases.

Cuban Exiles on the Trade Embargo

An Associated Press article of June 2004 by Anita Snow reports that Representative Ileana Ros-Lehtinen, a well-entrenched member of the conservative exiled Cuban community in Miami, welcomed the changes as a means of further denying Castro access to funds to finance his communist regime. Ms. Ros-Lehtninen believes that these new rules will "rob the dictatorship of funds to oppress the Cuban people."

On the other side of the fence, folks such as Miriam Leiva, wife of imprisoned dissident Oscar Espinosa Chepe, question the underlying motives of the Bush administration, as reported in *Salon*. "For which Cuba — and for whose Cuba — was the Bush administration's plan to hasten reform in Cuba written?"

How can restricting imprisoned Cubans — trapped in the island jail that Cuba has become — foster the fall of Fidel Castro? This new rule restricts access to basic items sent to Cubans on the island by their friends and family in the United States. I fail to understand how strangling the Cuban people, in a misguided attempt to foment an uprising, serves the good of the Cuban nation, at home and in exile, as well as the good of the United States. The American embargo on Cuba has been in place for over forty years with no positive change as a direct result. Fidel Castro remains firmly in power despite the embargo, or perhaps *due* to the embargo. How can dissident Cubans on the island meet with trusted family and friends to try to foment a revolution when basic needs are not satisfied? How can recruitment of counterrevolutionaries happen when the pool of potential recruits is nonexistent, as they are scouring the streets in an effort to *resolver*, to procure food, clothing, medicine and other necessities for themselves and their families?

Between United States policies and murderous deeds by Fidel Castro and his regime, the great majority of Cubans expend most, if not all, of their efforts in a daily race to survive. There is no time or energy for conspiring to create a counterrevolution, because all time and energy has to be spent in search of scoring the next meal, scoring heart medicine for their elderly parent or sickly child. All time and energy is spent on surviving. The new rules set by the Bush administration made it that much harder for Cubans in their daily lives. Fidel Castro and his party members will be unaffected by it, but will use it as one more example of the imperialist tendencies of the United States when Castro goes to other countries securing food and loans.

Travel and Funds

Limiting access of exiled Cubans to their friends and families back in Cuba has other implications. Limiting travel and the sending of goods and money directly limits the frequency of contact between exiled Cubans and those on the island. Each contact is an opportunity to showcase alternatives to Castro and his oppressive ways. Each contact is an opportunity to plant those *bombitas subversivas* mentioned earlier. What the new rules set by the current administration do is deny opportunities. Opportunities for the oppressed Cuban to decrease the stress and preoccupation of searching for basic goods, while providing a window into the future. A future without Fidel Castro and his oppressive regime. An attainable future. A future that includes a free and open society where basic human needs are met, while human rights are respected. A future with hope.

X

Padre Armando Llorente

In 1950s Cuba, as in times prior, it was not uncommon for families wishing to better the education of their sons to send these boys to live at Catholic boarding schools in Havana. This was even more true for those families that lived either in rural communities, or at great distances from Havana, as opportunities such as quality higher education tended to be centralized in the capital. The most eminent school of those times was named Belen (Bethlehem), a secondary school (high school) operated by Jesuit priests, a Catholic order that has a long and strong tradition of fostering academic and religious education throughout the world. As a child, having completed the sixth grade and primary school, Fidel Castro arrived to live at the Belen campus. Shortly afterward, a young Spanish seminarian, Armando Llorente, finalizing his studies to receive his priestly orders, also arrived to teach at Belen.

Cuba had seen in 1928 how these Jesuit priests, guided by Father Castro Rey as their director, established *La Agrupación Católica*, or the Catholic Grouping. This institution was founded to bring a greater religious and spiritual element into the students' daily lives, in family life at home and at Catholic schools and study centers. The priests directed their recruiting efforts toward young men and women attending high school or universities in Cuba, offering yearly spiritual retreats, daily mass, and other spiritual activities and seminars designed to foster the desire to learn and explore the Catholic faith. As these students married and their families grew, the scope of these groups became increasingly supportive of families and their attempts to maintain a Christ-centered way of life. This was not a unique endeavor to Cuba, but part of a worldwide effort that saw the establishment of numerous of these facilities throughout many countries, particularly in Latin America and the Caribbean nations. Father Castro Rey remained as director of La Agrupación until his death in 1950s. Following that event, Father Llorente, by then an ordained priest, was installed as the second director. These men and women, college students mostly, had felt a need to bring their lives closer to God, and worked to do so through their daily lives, work and studies. For some of these students, this need for exploring and strengthening their spiritual lives occurred as a response to the increasing communist ideology fermenting within their schools and universities.

As the second director, Father Llorente was an instrumental part of continuing this work of faith, a task he willingly took on back then in Cuba, and that he continues to this day in Miami. Following the ascent of Fidel Castro to power, coupled with subsequent religious persecution, La Agrupación was forced to close and cease its mission in Cuba, with most priests and religious expelled from the island, including this dynamic man of the cloth. Through his personal experiences in Cuba and later in his years in the United States, which number over four decades now, Father Llorente has seen the effects of the embargo, not only through personal experience, but also through the lives of his congregation. Prior to our meeting, I had been warned that he would probably not speak about his personal experiences with Castro, as an emissary of the Vatican sent to interview Castro in 1958 shortly before he took power.

Father Llorente is a Spanish Jesuit with a soft voice and soft features rising from a round face, unchanged over decades and easily mistaken for that of a younger man. As a seminarian, he was sent to Cuba from Spain by the director of his order to teach at Belen High School. His first year as an instructor coincided with Castro's first year there as a student, a fact of some importance later in his life. Following his initial three years, he returned to Spain to finish his theological studies and to become ordained as a Jesuit priest. This process took another three and one-half years, following which he found himself assigned back to Cuba to continue teaching at Belen in 1951.

The Vatican does not employ ambassadors to represent it throughout the world; instead their emissaries are called nuncio and are appointed by the Pope as representatives, enjoying the same diplomatic status as ambassadors. In 1958, seven years following Father Llorente's return to Cuba, the nuncio of the Vatican in Havana, Monsignor Luigi Centoz, received a written directive from the Vatican requesting further information on Castro and his revolution. Was this a Christian revolution as claimed by Castro? Was this a just revolution as proposed by others? Or was this truly a communist revolution as charged by yet others? The Vatican greatly desired an objective investigation and opinion of what was going on and had directed the nuncio to obtain it.

As the aging nuncio was not very familiar with Cuba outside of Havana, he approached the rector to the Jesuit priests at Belen High School with a plea for assistance. It appeared that Fidel Castro's last substantial contact with any Catholics had been with these priests while attending the Belen. Following that he had attended the increasingly agnostic and communist University of Havana, and subsequently fled to the Sierra Maestra Mountains as a fledgling revolutionist.

The rector, or director, at Belen, following the request by the nuncio, called in Father Llorente, showed him the Vatican's letter and asked for his assistance. Father Llorente explains, "The rector knew I had taught Fidel Castro in the recent past, called me in to meet with him and the nuncio, and explained the situation as they sought my opinion. I simply said that I would go. The rector asked if I was aware that I could be killed by either the governmental forces or by Castro's forces, to which I had replied by asking what was the difference if they killed me or another. I would go, but if I were to die, my only request would be that it would be published that I was there doing an investigation at the request of the church, not as a communist, not as a part of Castro's revolutionary forces." Father Llorente relates this in a casual manner, matter-of-fact, as if he had been asked to go to the bakery for bread. He was neither proud nor reluctant to comply with the request, he just saw it as part of what he was called to do as a priest, and, as a priest, was not afraid of death if that happened to be the path that God had chosen for him.

This amazing chapter in Father Llorente's life remains relatively closed. He readily states that he went, was treated fairly by all, and was obviously not killed or injured, but this was not a two-week vacation up in the Cuban mountains in 1958. It was a serious matter, from which a revolution and four decades of population attrition was begotten.

Father Llorente's face betrays him, clouding, as he states that "this is a chapter in my life that is not done ... yet, a chapter I am not ready to dwell [on] again at this time. Perhaps some day I may be able to." Out of respect for the gravity of the statement and the manner in which he obviously becomes uncomfortable with the recollection of that trip, I do not press him further, except to ask the outcome.

It turns out that Fidel Castro put on a show for him, as for all the world. He claimed to be the great Christian savior of Cuba, with masses of religious followers ready to fight and die with him to defeat a corrupt government, and yet to Father Llorente it was apparent that the reported revolutionary army he commanded did not exist. "That was not communism, nor Maoism, nor egoism, nor any of the subsequent labels that were given to his movement. It was all 'Fidelism.' By Fidel, for Fidel, and about Fidel." Castro at that time was everything to everyone who came within his realm, so long as he thought it would move his cause forward. He was willing to align himself with anyone he thought would make it possible for him to succeed, and he denied or embraced different positions as he saw fit.

I ask Father Llorente whether he thought that eventually Castro became a communist because it was the most convenient ideology for him and his plans of dictatorial rule of Cuba. To this he quickly replies, "Castro did not 'become' a communist, he simply relied upon communism to maintain power. Fidel's problem is about power, and communism was his only means of staying in power without elections." Llorente chuckles at this point he is making, leaving me to wonder if this has to do with knowing and investigating the self-proclaimed Christian savior of Cuba just to see him turn completely in an opposite direction and do whatever was needed to avoid elections, including embracing the atheist communist dogma.

"Cuba, you will notice, is the only country that is officially communistic, that has not killed a priest or a nun. In all the other ones they killed all the priests they could and all the nuns they could. *Hmph!*" Father Llorente seems disgusted at the thought of those who could kill men and women of the cloth. I am amazed at how quickly his kind and easygoing demeanor evaporate, replaced with anger and contempt so forceful it almost has a physical presence. Father Llorente was by no means attempting to score points for Fidel Castro; no, his disgust seemed to emanate from amazement at how not only were he and his colleagues treated poorly in Cuba, but in other countries summarily executed. This point, minor and personal as it appears to be, seems the pivotal evidence upon which Father Llorente sees the justification of his theory that deep within Fidel Castro there is not a communist, but a self-centered dictator. "Why, because Fidel is not a communist, he just uses communism for his ego."

Father Llorente asks for more of my questions as quickly as he finishes them. He is ready, raring to go, wanting to impart his wisdom, yet cautiously holding back at times. His rapid-fire way of speaking in heavily accented Spanish, quick hand gestures, expressive face, and heartfelt comments are typical of Spanish Jesuit priests. In the decades I have known him, he has been ready to go at a moment's notice, ready to jump into an intellectual foray or a soul-saving crusade, or begin prayerful thought and reflection with equal ease and facility. It is easy to see how the Spanish Christians were able to make forays into the newly discovered Americas centuries ago when a man like Father Llorente is met. It is easy to envision Spanish priests of those years following Columbus's accidental discovery readily boarding sailing vessels for parts unknown, driven by the thought that there was work to do, places to see, people to convert to Christianity.

"After the failure of the [Bay of Pigs] invasion, I had to leave for the United States. With the failure of the invasion, Fidel was emboldened to seize churches, schools and monasteries, expelling priests and nuns along the way. There were many members of *La Agrupación* that participated in the invasion." Catholic groups and associations such as *La Agrupación* had been under the scrutiny of Castro's minions for quite some time, and the failed invasion was the pinnacle event that provided Castro with an excuse to pursue these groups and associated members and families, to expel their religious leaders, and to seize any and all property remotely considered to be Catholic or religious.

Once Castro took over all of these facilities, Father Llorente found himself on the street, and rapidly fled to Miami with little more than a suitcase in hand. He was able to fly out of Cuba, since as a priest and a foreigner he was no longer welcomed. In fact, he was concerned at that time for his safety and life. Having a Spanish passport, an American visa, and friends and fellows from La Agrupación waiting for him in Miami, facilitated leaving Cuba. "There [were many] from *La Agrupación* already here in Miami when I arrived, as they had fled for fear of their lives and [those] of their families. I accepted that I could lead them spiritually here [in Miami] or in Cuba, so we reestablished ourselves in Miami."

Following his arrival in Miami, Father Llorente set out to reestablish *La Agrupación*, which he was able to do. Since the 1960s they have occupied a small campus just north of downtown Miami along Biscayne Bay.

The graceful buildings are of the Spanish Mediterranean architecture so prevalent throughout Florida. The lush subtropical landscape is, enhanced by numerous religious plaques and statues that grace the grounds. This community of the faithful includes priests and laity whom have taken a vow to be an "associate," a quasi-religious role. Associates are unlike priests in that they do not share in the religious sacrament, yet these folks have also dedicated their lives to Christ.

The buildings include residences, a modest office, and a chapel. The chapel was beautifully redone in the early sixties at the behest of Father Llorente, employing the architectural talents of my father. If I am sound biased as to the beauty and features of this modest chapel, it is because I am. The proof is that the chapel remains in daily use, and is as spiritually comforting today, as it was in the sixties when my brother and I were altar boys assisting the mass at this chapel. Of all the projects my father has designed, built, or otherwise participated in, this remains, in my eyes, his masterpiece, the pinnacle of his career. The love and care are evident through the simple, thoughtful designs reflecting his faith, such as curved pews centered toward the altar. These pews were a source of much debate among parishioners at the time of construction, until the idea behind the curvature was finally understood: the pews were curved and centered toward the altar as a gesture of recognition of Christ as the ultimate teacher, and, in turn, the congregation, his students, gathered to hear and receive his teachings on the pews. Any artist, artisan, or architect should be so lucky to have one project such as this in a lifetime.

As more members of *La Agrupación* fled Cuba and filled these pews, the effects of the embargo became more evident. Families were unable to remain in touch. Parents sent their children to the United States, with the hope and prayer that they would be cared for and that they would be eventually reunited, only to have those hopes dashed. The chapel remains much the same as in the 1960s. A few added items are noted: a plaque with a piece of the demolished Berlin Wall, and a handmade cross.

The cross is an interesting item. It was carved from wood salvaged from cigar boxes. It is beautifully detailed, inlaid with scenes of the Stations of the Cross. When asked about its origin, Father Llorente explains that it was made by members of *La Agrupación* who had been captured during the Bay of Pigs fiasco and were awaiting execution. As a sign of their faith, these men secretively carved this cross in Fidel Castro's bar-

baric jail: the cross survived, along with some of the men, when President Kennedy negotiated their release and exile to the US, just hours prior to the scheduled execution of those surviving. Kennedy also secured the release and return of the bodies of those who had already been executed. This was an act by Kennedy to "attempt to settle his conscious for betraying the Cubans at Bay of Pigs," as Father sees it.

Exiting the chapel, our conversation returns to the embargo and the affects it has had upon the community. Father Llorente initially maintains that he does not know much about the embargo, but then readily discusses its nature and effects.

"At that time of my arrival [in Miami], the embargo, or at least the effect of the embargo, was not in place. This embargo is a disgrace. It is a problem that is mostly one of political and social consequences." Llorente continues, occasionally pounding the table to emphasize his points as he wonders how the United States can place an embargo while all of its trading partners can continue to trade with Cuba, either directly or through Canada and Mexico. "The embargo is another American pretext—" For once Llorente appears to have lost his train of thought, but quickly recovers: "The embargo is one of those Solomonic decisions by the United States, as the Biblical figure, trying to split the child." Father Llorente pounds the table with each example: "Germany: in half!" (Bam!) " Korea: in half!" (Bam!) "Vietnam: in half!" (Bam!) "These are half decisions that are worthless." (Bam, bam, bam!) This last pounding seems to even catch Father Llorente by surprise, but onward he continues: "If the United States truly wants an embargo, it should do it. Make a total blockage. Block the isle from the world, and that's it."

His fist is back again, banging the table to drive home his points. I can't help but smile at each thump. I am not sure why I find myself smiling; perhaps it is merely in response to the passion and emotion flowing from this priest. Llorente claims to not be in tune with the embargo, to not know much about it, but it is plainly evident that he is outraged by the stupidity of it, and the devastating effects it has on an innocent population.

Llorente relates the issues and travesty of the embargo to the suffering of Christ. He is amazed at the manner in which history appears to repeat itself, as political decisions are made by those in power without thought of their consequences or profound impact. Llorente can see how the embargo, as a political tool of the US, does nothing more than entrench Castro in power at the expense of all Cubans.

"The problem of Fidel Castro is ... grave. It is like a cancer. Do we operate and remove the cancer, or do we not? At this point it appears as if the plan is to let him die whenever he dies, as the least controversial solution. There appears to be nothing, nothing, nothing, *nothing*, being truly done to solve the issue of the embargo."

Llorente continues discussing the embargo and how it has been manipulated. He states that Castro declared himself a mortal enemy of the US, and will endeavor to keep the embargo in place. It is ironic for him how the amount of money that the exiled Cubans send to Cuba every year greatly surpasses the amount Cuba loses to the embargo.

I find that to be an interesting point, one that does not fail to catch my attention every time I hear someone mention how they send money back to Cuba to support their friends or relatives. Yes, it is difficult not to want to help your family in need, but why not look at the big picture: help liberate the country, and that in turn will help your suffering relative. The same people — the exiled Cuban community, living mostly in Miami, who endeavor to keep this embargo in place, at seemingly any cost — are one of the main reasons why the embargo is a failed policy. They are blind to the irony of how much energy they expend to maintain the embargo, yet little by little, dollar by dollar, all the *envíos* of money to Cuba undermine and defeat the alleged purpose of the embargo as a mean of punishing Castro and liberating Cuba. The embargo can be seen as a dam, holding back the waters of the world from Cuba, but the *envíos* are each a leak, collectively rendering this dam a sieve. It may be that there is such an emotionally powerful reaction and desire to do something, to punish Castro, that it blinds an entire community to the point where it cannot see how it is defeating itself.

"You can close all the sugar mills in Cuba and the impact will be minimal. This exiled community sends money that eventually ends up supporting those that stole their lands and assets. Can you *imagine* that? What a dramatic comedy. Castro stole it all, and lived from the ill-gotten fruit for twenty-plus years. Once that was exhausted, he has allowed the exiled community to maintain him. But there is no way that it would have happened another way, because, for all their faults, Cubans are a big-hearted people and could not allow to see their families suffer and starve."

Father Llorente sees the embargo as not much more than a "feel good" measure by the United States, created and continued so that it seems as if it is doing something. Yet he repeats that the embargo benefits no one, with the exception of Castro. He makes the point that this is a complicated issue, further complicated by the exiled Cuban community that would never allow a dismantling of the embargo. And yet, that is also seen as a lie, or perhaps as a pacifier.

"The community, the exiled Cuban community here, is living a lie. It is allowed to keep the embargo, thinking that it is something significant for them to have to fight Castro, because they are not allowed [by the US] to do anything else. The exiled Cubans could easily create and enforce a blockade of Cuba with five fast boats. But they are "not allowed" [one of many] lies. Lies like the Cuban missile crises. It was all an excuse to rein in the exiled Cubans while [cementing] Fidel Castro into power. Part of the deal with the Americans and Soviets over Cuba was that the United States would not allow anyone to attack or invade Cuba. The United States will stop, and has stopped, anyone that is attempting to stage a removal of Castro from power. These exiled Cubans are not allowed, and would be militarily denied the right to attempt a change in government in their own country. This is such a mess, an incredible mix that doesn't make sense. An *arroz con mangos.*"

"Arroz con Mangos" is one of those colloquial Cuban expressions. It translates as "rice with mangoes," and it used to identify a mix that is so unusual that no one touches (or eats) it.

"Look at the embargo from a practical point of view and you will see that it is nothing, although it has the appearance of being something. The embargo also fails due to the leftist community in this country. Look at Venezuela today; the United States could do so much for them, help those folks stabilize and prosper, but instead it chooses to ignore them for now. The United States is so powerful that with its pinky it can do those things that others just dream about. But it does not use that power wisely, nor with true compassion. The United States follows policies that will benefit the United States only. No matter what it says, it is doing what is best for them."

We have been sitting facing each other at a wooden picnic table underneath a pavilion, enjoying the breeze, along with the relative coolness of a March day in Miami. The tabletop serves as an instrument to resonate

Llorente's pounding fist as he emphasizes words, thoughts and sentiments. Airplanes leaving Miami International Airport, flying almost directly over-head, occasionally interrupt our peaceful setting, as do the sounds of traffic from Biscayne Boulevard that occasionally drift our way. The rest of the time we hear the rhythmic lapping of choppy waves on the sea wall, the distinct swish of palm trees swaying their fronds in the breeze, and the intermittent hum of air conditioning units as they kick on, for coolness in Miami is a relative term. I am pleased at this opportunity to speak with Father Llorente, because I have known him for so long, and can trust that what he says will be frank.

The silver lining that Llorente sees to the embargo and Castro's iron-fisted grasp of power is, not surprisingly, a religious one. While families do suffer for their loved ones in Cuba, and those in Cuba live a horrible life as a result of these policies, he believes that the average Cuban family in Miami has benefited from living in the United States. These benefits are not only of material wealth, but also spiritual wealth.

In the Cuba that Father Llorente knew, "The husband rarely went to church, with the possible exception of weddings, baptisms, first communions and funerals. Religion and church was a thing of the women. The Cubans in exile have become much more religious than their counterparts in Cuba, or if they had stayed the course, pre-Castro, although religion was on the rise in Cuba. There were some very good Christian groups forming, and a much better understanding and support of the church was evolving. But just as it was truly starting to gain momentum, it was derailed by the revolution. The exiled Cuban has not only benefited from this country [the US], but has provided a wealth of benefits for this country."

Father Llorente sees the problems and issues of Cuba as a plan of God that is long-term, a plan that to be initiated must yet wait. People, singularly, or collectively as a nation, will not commence to reform themselves and pull themselves up until they hit the bottom of the pit.

"The Cubans on the island are a great mess from a spiritual point. But there is hope, as there appears to be a grassroot resurgence of faith: a truly Catholic and Christian resurgence born from the relentless persecution and misery. The future is hard to predict, but I think it will be good for Cuba. The material aspects of resurgence will outshine that of what happened with the reunification of Germany, but all that will pale in comparison to the spiritual resurgence that will emerge [within] five or so years once Castro is dead and gone. People are tired of living the lies and falseness. People are tired of Fidel and all that he represents, all his lies, all his falseness. Castro has a lot of abilities, and by his standards has accomplished a lot. But he is incapable of loving, and cannot love Cubans."

We discuss Fidel Castro further, then Father Llorente makes an interesting comment. He shares with me how some Cubans have confided in him, saying that "part of the problem with Castro, why he continues to be misinterpreted so much by Americans and others, alike, is that Castro is not a real Cuban. He is a *Gallego* from *Galicia*, a region in Spain where people have great talent with commerce and business, but Castro has instead misused that talent to hurt others and make them suffer because he had such a tragic beginning. His mother was his dad's servant, and that has haunted him all his life. All he cares about is remaining in power. He battled those demons while in Belen, but in the end was unable to conquer them. These insecurities have affected his psyche, have driven him to extremes that perhaps he would not have otherwise obtained. [Being] the son of a chambermaid whose boss [was] his father has profoundly affected [him]."

The picture that Father Llorente is providing me appears to be of a Castro who was given a lot of love and encouragement in school and elsewhere — he was a good and capable student, very smart, and always trying hard to excel — but his driving force was not love, not even love of knowledge, but hatred. Father Llorente continues to verbalize his thoughts:

> He loves a good fight, and the embargo is a good fight for him. Remove the embargo and he will lose validity, but he will look for other fights, other ways to continue in power, other ways to blame his failures. Cuba has so much richness it could live a good life, if Castro had just done one thing: installed an honest government. The problem with ... Cuba prior to Castro was [that] the corruption was so great that you had to be stupid to be in a governmental office and not make money. Politics had been so perverted he could have fixed all of that, but his problem is power. Fidel needs to be in power, and without a dictatorship he would have had to share power, which he was unwilling to do. A shame, a true shame, for Cuba could have been a very prosperous nation by now. And this sham of embargo, once again, does not accomplish much more than keep Castro in power at the expense and suffering of the people.
>
> Look how other nations do invest in the little bit of tourism that Cas-

tro allows: the Canadians, the English, Mexican, French, and Spaniards. They see that this was a rich country and can be rich again. It has sugar, cattle, mining resources, and such. All wasted by Castro in his quest for power and more power. Castro has always been about power. Not drugs; not women; just power. All those people worth anything cannot stand to be next to Fidel, and therefore mediocre people surround him. Fidel Castro is an overgrown, spoiled child, says one thing today, the opposite tomorrow — whatever pleases his fancy. He lives from his lunacy; it is all about him, and all else be damned.

Father Llorente finishes our conversation, inquiring as to how the material will be used, which leads us to talk about how a research paper grew. I share with him how most exiled Cubans, in private are eventually willing to admit that the embargo is a failure. With the exception of some who are so simpleminded that they need to have political ideology prefabricated for them by their leaders, most Cubans are smart and compassionate enough to see how a policy created and maintained with the supposed intent of bringing a dictator to his knees has been a total failure.

As I leave the beautiful compound and walk to my car, failing to avoid a vagrant, so ever present in Miami, who sees my camera and offers to take pictures for me, my thoughts are engulfed with the thoughts and images of Castro's Cuba and how a stubborn attitude of the US government can survive year after year, through different administrations with widely varying ideologies. The skies have been clouding during the time Father Llorente and I have been speaking. The grayness mirrors my thoughts of what the broken spirit of Cubans must be. I recollect one of Llorente's analogies on the embargo as a solution to the problem of Fidel Castro.

"This is a solution that is not a solution. Just as what happened to Christ with Pilate, who wanted to save [him]. But what did he do? Sent him to Herrod which was not a solution, who compared him to Barrabás, which was not a solution, and flogged him, which was not a solution." With each comparison, Father's voice drops, to where it is almost a whisper, a mournful whisper filled with the love for Christ and the pain for the suffering endured on the cross. "And finally, he handed him over. The same story repeats itself. These half solutions do not work at all, and history repeats itself. The embargo needs to be looked at carefully. Look to see who is trading with Cuba. It is a pretext, a pretext for Fidel Castro. The embargo is a tool for Castro to use to continue to justify his dictatorship. Fidel blames all that goes wrong in Cuba on the embargo. Even the Holy Pope [told Castro] to 'drop it.' The embargo enables Fidel Castro to obtain loans and financing to maintain his fragile economy, as he continues to blame the United States for all his woes."

XI

Cullowhee Methodist Church

Exiled Cubans have been dispersed throughout the world and, in particular, the US. Outside of South Florida and the northeastern United States, most enjoy a cordial, if not gracious relationship with the majority of Americans they interact with in their daily lives and travels. Cubans are found in all fifty states, and by their presence alone have fostered a continued interest in Cuba among community members. Churches, as is their nature, have been particularly sensitive to the trials and hardships suffered by Cubans under Castro. This has led to relief efforts initiated by numerous church groups, associations, and affiliated individuals. And if a soul or two is converted and saved — better yet.

One of Fidel Castro's unexplainable quirks has been his inclination to allow varying degrees of freedom for religious worship within Cuba. Religious services in Cuba are infrequent, yet well attended, even though they are monitored and documented by the state police. Theories abound as to why Castro has allowed religious activities to continue and, in some recent years, increase. Could it be the need for US dollars that religious groups bring in? Could it be that as Castro's formative years were spent in Catholic schools there is a sliver of respect or fear of God left in him? Could these be the beginnings of overtures to get himself right with God as the relentless advancement of age takes its toll upon him? There are many more theories as numerous as all the pundits on Miami's fervent radio talk shows, but they are guesses, at best.

In the small community of Cullowhee, nestled in gorgeous western North Carolina, there is a vibrant Methodist church which has taken up as one of its many causes the need of Cuban children for medical supplies. This particular congregation has a long-standing tradition of service to the community, as exemplified by numerous organizations that depend on their generosity and accessibility for their meeting facilities to conduct business or fulfill their missions. These include Cub Scouts, Boy Scouts, immigrant groups, and many others. It is known among the members of the community at large that, if you have a group that needs a meeting locale, the Cullowhee Methodist Church can always be counted on to make space for you.

The Cuban service project is mainly the undertaking of the church's youth group and its adult leaders. In 2004 alone, they collected, packaged, shipped and distributed over $250,000 in medical supplies, augmented with some musical instruments. The medical supplies were mostly provided to the rural children's medical center in Varadero, Cuba, while the musical instruments were donated to Varadero's Methodist Church.

The adult leaders of the group are a middle-aged couple, Norman West and his wife, Carol. I have had the pleasure of knowing Norman through mutual interactions in the community; Norman enjoys a highly successful real estate and home building business here. Born and raised in High Point, North Carolina, Norman moved to Cullowhee in 1964 to attend Western Carolina University, during which time he met his wife. Subsequently he never left, but established roots, family and a business in the area. Typical of southerners, he is a devout Christian, and dedicates a good portion of his time and effort to his church community, as well as to the community at large. Interacting with Norman usually involves a congenial exchange, splattered with bursts of energy, and accentuated with the southern laissez-faire outlook toward life. A soft drawl laces an authoritative voice and demeanor, yet this gentleman will not negate you, or your opinion or ideals. He has mastered the art of listening, and has the decisiveness and energy needed to carry thoughts to fruition. Piercing blue eyes sparkle and dance with life and energy, their intensity increasing with conversations invoking subjects near and dear to him: church, family, and, in particular, the youth group. These eyes are framed in a tanned, rounded face that retains youthful vigor. A balding head is surrounded by collar-length hair, evoking his college days in the 1960s, like a favorite professor or uncle. Norman seems to genuinely care about those he comes in contact with, be it through business, church, or life in general.

Through Norman's religious circles, he came to know a fellow by the name of Larry Corbin (not his real name), with an organization called *A World Foundation* (not its real name). This foundation is dedicated to alleviating the medical crises in Cuba, in particular those of children. A predicament has been created and compounded by an embargo that, despite its exclusions for humanitarian issues, has created a chronic short-age of durable medical goods, as well as a shortage of everyday supplies, such as crutches, IV start kits, bandages, and sterile dressings, items we take for granted here in the US. Imagine traveling abroad and falling ill, or, worse, having your child become ill. You take her to the hospital for what should be a routine procedure, such as an appendectomy. The appen-dix has to be removed, otherwise it will rupture and kill your child. Here in the US this would be a "no brainer," a procedure so routine the child is home the following day, if not the same day. In Cuba you would run a higher risk of secondary infections, due to the acute scarcity of medical supplies. Imagine being the doctor or nurse forced to ration precious sup-plies on a daily basis. Who will get the bandages? Who will get IV fluids? Who may force a higher risk of infections and complications, while her roommate recuperates and is discharged without any incident? It is sce-narios such as these, real scenarios that occur daily in Cuba as a result of the embargo, that have motivated people such as Norman West and Larry Corbin.

I walk into Norman's office one fall day, to chat with him a while about his last trip to Cuba, taken in the summer of 2004. His office building is located in the heart of the closest thing to a downtown or business dis-trict that Cullowhee possesses. There is one flashing light at the back entrance to Western Carolina University; otherwise there are no traffic lights in this part of town. The Tuckasegee River flows peacefully nearby, accentuated by the newly arriving colors displayed on the trees. The air temperature has dropped a degree or two this morning as a cold front moves in, bringing wind and rain. Norman's office is located on the ground floor of a two-story mixed-use building crowned with apartments. Warm stone sides the facade, trimmed in wood, well-kept for its years, inviting and unpretentious, much like Norman.

We start by discussing how he became involved in missionary trips. Coffee from a thermos is produced and poured, sweetened with Kahlua. As we sip the coffee and begin to chat, he leans back in his chair and props his feet on his desk.

"Well," begins Norman, "my friend Larry Corbin started going to Cuba as a curiosity thing and snuck in, one of the many ways you can sneak in, through the Dominican Republic or Mexico or something like that. He met a girl who is a nurse, and got involved with her activities, and her main activity was working at a pediatric cancer hospital. Through her he became involved with the children and their plight. Their plight is pretty remorseful. So Larry said, 'Hell, I'm going to see if I can't do something about this,' [and] started smuggling supplies into Cuba in his suitcase, some as basic as ... aspirin." Norman recounts how Larry's efforts were quickly enhanced by members of his home community and church, which led to an organization being formed, to be able to donate a larger volume of supplies to the hospital, more than just one or two suitcases-full each trip. Norman's first visit to Cuba was to accompany Larry with a shipping container stocked with donated medical supplies. That trip was the impetus that gave Norman the idea to bring his youth group to Cuba. The group took almost two years raising money to buy the supplies they would take with them to donate to the hospital. Fourteen people traveled to Cuba, all but three being young adults, seniors at the local high school.

This service project provides a glimpse at one of Norman's character traits, that of doing things as well as possible. "In years past we have gone to Kentucky, migrant camps in Florida; we rehabbed houses in Savannah, Georgia; we've done the typical kind of things that most church youth groups do.... Carol, my wife, and I are the directors of the Senior High Youth Program [at Cullowhee Methodist Church], and we both got involved, like most people do, because or son was in it. So we did it for four years — we ran his youth group for four years. Anyway, I wanted to end it [his tenure as director] on a big note, but, boy, it was a lot of trouble; I'm not sure I would do it again." Norman laughs heartily with that thought, a broad smile giving away the secret that, if asked, he would do it again. "I can't tell you how glad I am I did it. I am going again in January, but just to help Larry."

The coffee with Kahlua is rather good, its warmth gratefully received on this cool day. We turn our conversation more toward politics and Cuba. As the wind starts to blow again outside, Norman drops his feet from the edge of his desk, leans forward, and declares that while he does profess to understand politics, and keeps up with up with them as much as possible, when it comes to American politics and Cuba, "I don't understand ... I believe that the history just repeats itself. Government and world leaders do dumb things, time and again. So — and — well, I don't care to do dumb things." Here Norman's usually laid-back demeanor gives way to anger. His face sharpens and his voice drops. "Especially when these dumb things cost human lives and things like that. An economic embargo may even be good for the Cuban people; I'll tell you why in just a minute. But, when an embargo is keeping medicine from little babies, you know that is not fair. That is inhumane. They [the world leaders] will have to answer to that one of these days. That [embargo] is one of the dumbest things I have ever heard; it causes human suffering and I just can't believe that that goes on."

Norman recounts how several of the kids who went on this trip were so incensed by the impact the embargo has on Cubans that upon their return they collectively wrote several letters to members of Congress and to the president. "Several of our kids wrote letters to George Bush to tell him 'you better get down to this hospital for a few hours, and then you'd do away with the embargo.'"

Returning to his previous statement that the embargo may benefit Cubans in some ways, Norman laughs, props his feet back up on the desk, and says, "A lot of ... Americans feel sorry for the Cubans because they don't have SUVs and air conditioning, and they are not out every night partying, eating and spending money. But, the average Cuban lives over two years longer than the average American. They are healthier, they don't have our bad habits, and, despite needing a lot of things, they are pretty happy people." Norman adds, "Like most people in the world, Cubans do want more, and they do deserve more. But the embargo is terrible, although just because they don't live or dress like we do may not be as important as we may think it is."

During the two trips that Norman has made, he has noticed that the effects of the embargo are not equally felt by all Cubans. "Those people in power — the closer to Fidel you get, the better you live. When I first went to Cuba we had dinner one night at a local official's house. We ate duck that he had shot earlier that day with his beautiful antique shotgun. He had gone hunting with his two matching, well-trained black labs, hunting dogs. Those are luxuries most [Cuban] people don't have. And looking around his house, he obviously didn't lack for much, had a new Chevy truck in the garage, and apparently traveled abroad quite often. He may not have lived like a United States senator in the United States. By American standards they may not live too well, but they do have better houses, better cars, and they have access to better things."

"The average guy lives very differently. I was invited into several homes, and I remember one guy who was as proud as he could be to offer us coffee. That was all he had; he didn't even have bread to offer us. We also went to a wonderful man's house — Pedro, a retired minister — and you can tell he blew a big wad on the meal. But it was just vegetables and fruit. No meat, no wine, nothing like that. He was very gracious, just a very nice fellow. As we were leaving I thanked him, told him he was very gracious and that I was indebted to him. Know what he said? He said '*No señor*, *I* am the one who is indebted to all Americans, especially those from High Point, North Carolina.'"

Norman was flattered and puzzled. How could it be that this man knew he was originally from High Point? He asked, and the reply was equally surprising for Norman. Pedro, whose last name Norman would not give for fear of compromising his safety, had attended college and seminary school at High Point College many years ago, long before Fidel Castro. "That was a Methodist seminary back in the old days. It turned out that everywhere I go ... people know this fellow. He roomed with our former district superintendent in the Methodist church here. Tales about this guy are legendary. What a small world. Yet look how he had to live."

Signs of the embargo would present themselves far and wide to Norman throughout his trip. "We went to the national library. I like books, so I always seek libraries. Well, they didn't have any books in it. I'm not sure how libraries work down there, for here you can go into our libraries and just look through the books. In Cuba, you walk into that library and ask for the book you want, and they tell you whether or not you can get it. I went over to the card catalogue, apparently accessible by everybody, and I pulled out a drawer to find only about two inches ... of cards. Not only that, there [were] only two [units] of them, about three foot by three foot. [There weren't] a whole lot of card catalogues. Someone quickly told me to leave that thing alone. So I am not sure what the purpose of that library was. Yet we were able to go to an open air, black market book place that had thousands of titles."

Religious freedom also presented some contradictions to Norman as he traveled in Cuba. Norman believes that Castro gave some limited religious freedom back to the Cubans to appease them and retain control over them. Every service that Norman attended in Cuba was held at locations filled to capacity, with anxious worshipers spilling out to the steps, sidewalk and even streets. "But this could be because there are not very many open churches to begin with. As you ride around Cuba, you don't see many churches, definitely not even as many as here in Jackson County. But those that are open for service are filled quickly. There is some religious activity; [I] wouldn't call it freedom. We went to places far from Havana; we went to Varadero, Santa Clara, and many more remote places. We were accompanied by Pedro, who is well-known throughout Cuba." Throughout his travels Norman saw and experienced services provided by many different religions. A large number of these were given by missionary groups from the US and Korea. All of these were well attended by Cubans, in particular by children. "There seems to be a great need, a desire to hear the word of God in Cuba. Atheism may be the official religion, but you can give services down there."

It could be that Castro allows this since there is a significant amount of cash infused into the local Cuban economy with each of these groups. Norman agrees, "Oh, yes. Americans, at least those like us, doing the runs of missionaries and there to help, as opposed to those other 'tourists' [referring to those traveling to Cuba, in particular, to Havana, for the sex trade] ... were well-received. But I didn't go there to act like a rich American butt hole. I told my kids to not wear their best clothes, to leave their jewelry at home; I told them not to show off, not to throw their money around. I can't begin to tell you how well we were received. But we also brought a lot to give out, and so we were sought out too. Everywhere we went and spent money, we all bought stuff to bring home or to give away, well, everywhere I saw an open cash register that had American dollars in it. I couldn't even tell you what the Cuban money looks like."

"A friend of mine, his brother went to Cuba, snuck in through Puerto Rico or some other place. Well he's a big party boy, so he went and spent two weeks chasing women, drinking and doing drugs. So my friend asked me about my trip, and I had just spent a week there with all those kids, going to Methodist churches and events. When I was done he said, 'Dang, between the two of you, it sounds like you went to two different countries.'"

While in Cuba, Norman asked the people he encountered, at least those who were willing to chat, how they felt about Americans. He found that all told him basically the same thing, that Cubans do not hate Americans, and see the embargo as "a Bush-Castro thing." Norman says, "The people ... I asked may not be representative of all of Cuba, as my experience is that most Cubans are Christians, but that may not hold true out in the bush. The Methodists are the fasting growing religion in Cuba; they have abandoned the old-timey services, and instead have a lot of music, singing, clapping. Very charismatic. Drives the old guys like Pedro nuts; he waits until all that singing is done before he enters to preach. But he realizes it is bringing people into the church, and so he deals with it. I saw the [Methodist] bishop came to a service, and he got up there, clapping his hands and stomping his feet. But he sees the writing on the wall, and knows he needs to do this. But not Pedro; he'd just stay outside until the preaching started, as he thought [the music] was ruining it."

The religious institutions that Norman and his group interacted with in Cuba were all struggling. Struggling to remain solvent, to accommodate the needs of those who attend, struggling to survive. Some rent their facilities to other groups, mostly foreign missionaries, usually of any denomination, as long as there is compensation. Others seek direct donations of needed items made scarce by the embargo.

The Cuban Methodist Church sponsored Norman's group, as humanitarian visas are no longer allowed under new Bush administration rules; therefore they were able to receive religious visas. But the sponsorship came with a price. Most of the donations Norman and his kids took to Cuba were intended for the children's hospital, their original sponsor until the Bush administration canceled the humanitarian visas. Now they also had to deliver some of the donations to the church, and the church intended to receive the lion's share of it. Since the original intent of the group was to give the items to the hospital, a compromise was found, and the great majority of the items, almost all the medical supplies, went to the hospital, while the other items, such as musical instruments and toiletries, went to the church group.

The day that the items were distributed at the pediatric hospital, a sense of festivity prevailed, according to Norman. "You'd [have] thought we threw a party, which, in a sense, we did. The donated items were much-needed and well-received. The items given to the church were loaded, upon our arrival at the airport, into a lady's car, and by the time we got to the church's office a couple hours later, they were all gone. Life in Cuba must be rough."

Returning to life in Cuba, Norman informed me that while there he noticed that "most of the people do not mention Castro or speak about him, except perhaps in passing. You never hear anybody being critical of him. As he has the different echelons of police, there seems to be a great control over the people. You have the local cops, [who] walk up and down the street. They are very user-friendly. Then there is … the highway patrol, except they are not highway patrol. These people just stand around and watch stuff. And then there [are] government cops that come in. When we went to a hospital and threw a big party and gave them a lot of medicine … it happened that Larry [forgot] his briefcase [there]. Maybe an hour had transpired by the time we had left and he noticed it was gone and returned. When he walked in the room, the government people were already there going through all the bags of the donations. They obviously know every detail of what is going on in their country. We must have given 100,000 hypodermic needles, and they inspected each and every one of them."

But control of items in Cuba can be selective. Norman says that Larry Corbin is planning a follow-up trip for which he "has 2 shipping containers already full of supplies and equipment. Some really expensive equipment, X-ray machines and stuff like that. Now, he went and met with the government officials, because he was seeking some sort of acknowledgement; he wanted a guarantee that the equipment was not going to be placed on the black market or shipped to Africa. They wouldn't do it. They told him there no way they could guarantee that."

But that leads us to their economy, [in] which Castro assigns jobs to people. Some are very menial, [which] might be to keep one street, from corner to corner … clean…. They are given a little contraption, with dustpan and broom and a can. So everyone just throws trash on the ground, 'cause they know there is going to be a guy every thirty feet picking it up. That has to do with the fact that the government promises you a job, and you get a little paycheck. Anna, the secretary at the church, makes $7.50 a month. The monthly paychecks are very inadequate, and people strive to find other means of income. Everyone spends the eight hours a day they work for the government planning for the job they go to at night, or to the scam they run. In the better neighborhoods, people have converted their porches to little cafes [and] bars, where you can get little shots of rum, whiskey, or dinner. You can find homemade ice cream. Every other person sells cigars. A huge underground business. In Varadero they prevent panhandlers. So at the outskirts of town [are] the vendor markets and the panhandlers. Everybody carpools, but they make $7.75 a month [and] gas is $5 a gallon, and they are riding around town. So they all pool their money to go places. As we were unloading from our bus at one of the towns, a guy was standing there and drew my picture, and that of my wife and son … together, on some cardboard. In the five minutes it took me to give instructions to the kids, he did this; *then* he asked for a dollar for it, which I gladly gave to him. Turned out to be a good souvenir.

We heard rumors that the scams at the clubs at night are massive, but I don't really know anything about it, because we didn't go to the clubs. Every little town has a hot club with bands, music, alcohol, women — you name it. But again, I never saw a cash register open that wasn't full of dollars. The dollars, which aren't allowed down there, [are] the backbone of the whole economy."

Norman and I discussed how, if the embargo wasn't in effect, Cubans would be able to trade freely with anyone, including the United States. That would perhaps improve the economic situation of the great majority, in turn leading to a greater demand for goods. This, in turn, says Norman, "as they wish for a better lot in life, could cause them to get rid of the government, of Castro, in order to be able to live a better life. For some reason, they don't seem to have many appliances. They are hard to get and are terribly expensive. There [are] no clothing stores, but everyone has clothes. I don't understand it; I just know they are good people and should have better."

Where do Cubans' funds come from? If it is not from illegal or extracurricular activities, "scams," as Norman calls them, then obviously the support from the exile community is what sustains people. This support amounts to well over $800 million a year, a sizeable amount, especially when you consider it is "free" money. The folks sending $20, $30, $50, or $100 to their relatives expect nothing in return, no trade, no goods, and no services. This money flowing out of the US is charity, in other words. This money is critical to the survival of those who receive it, without which they would be in total misery. Yet the Bush administration is proposing to restrict this, under the pretense of "strengthening the embargo." Why? It will not affect those in power, who will continue to live well, eat well, go abroad, and hunt with their favorite antique shotgun, with matching dogs at their side.

The embargo maintains that reality as the status quo. Over forty-five years of the embargo have not occasioned the removal of Castro or the Communist Party from power in Cuba. Basic human rights there range from nonexistent to few. Castro and his cronies remain entrenched, and will perhaps leave power only when they are carried out by pallbearers. Millions of ordinary, God-fearing, God-starved people suffer. Is it not time we try a different tactic?

I had the privilege of being invited to present my thoughts and information on Cuba to the young men and women of the senior youth group at Cullowhee Methodist Church. As the church is located adjacent to the campus of Western Carolina University, many of these youth come from homes headed by professors and other well-educated staff of the university.

Norman West invited me to come speak to them as a means of preparing them for their upcoming missionary trip to Cuba. As we discussed issues related to Cuba and the policies of the United States, it became very evident that here was a diverse group of young Americans, all with apparent thirst for knowledge about Cuba. These folks presented thoughtful questions and observations about how the US can affect such a "lesser" country as Cuba. As Americans, we are wealthy compared to many of our immediate neighbors, and that wealth extends beyond material goods: we have a wealth of freedoms that appear to be taken for granted here. These are the same freedoms that are severely restricted, if even available, in many of our neighboring countries.

For me, as both an American and the son of Cuban immigrants, it was encouraging to realize that in small communities, and gatherings as insular as a small Appalachian church youth group, there are embodied some of the qualities that make the United States great: empathy and generosity toward those less fortunate — the needy, those who are truly suffering — coupled with the desire and self-motivation needed to actually assist. Perhaps a change in how we choose to display our displeasure with Fidel Castro's communist antics could facilitate Castro's removal or demise. This might allow a more complementary exchange of goods, people, services and resources in a manner that embodies our American principles, while respecting Cuba's sovereignty. If the young men and women from this youth group understand this, perhaps, through their good deeds, they will be able to initiate the changes needed.

XII

NPR

REACTION TO AN INTERVIEW
WITH ELOY GUTIERREZ-MENOYO

Despite the accusations to the contrary, I have found that National Public Radio (NPR) attempts to disseminate as balanced a newscast as possible. I refuse to affiliate with one party or the other, as I like to develop my own convictions and not blindly follow those created for a platform. With the schedule that I tend to have, coupled with my belief in no television at home, I rely on radio, the Internet, and news magazines.

On February 14, 2005, as I drove to Florida from North Carolina, I happened to hear an interview by Lourdes Garcia-Navarro (on NPR's "All Things Considered"). In this interview, Garcia-Navarro examined how a Cuban dissident faced possible criminal prosecution, and another ten years of jail time for his anti–Castro activities and travel.

Garcia-Navarro explained that the Spanish native Eloy Gutierrez-Menoyo, a citizen of the US living in Havana, was a past *castrista* who fought alongside Castro, as so many other Cubans have, only to change his mind about Castro, and to fight against him, for which he had to serve 22 years in a Cuban prison, following a failed insurrection.

Gutierrez-Menoyo is a *dialóguelo*, seeking to promote change through dialogue with the Cuban government, an ideal that has earned him the mistrust of most fellow dissidents in Cuba. For this he is also lambasted by exiled Cubans, such as Frank Calzón of the Center for a Free Cuba, who states, "[Mr. Gutierrez-Menoyo] has chosen ... a wrong strategy to deal with Mr. Castro. He is trying to engage Castro very much on Castro's terms."

In his NPR interview, Gutierrez-Menoyo explained how he was seeking an independent line of opposition in an attempt to bring change to Cuba. As he was not following the approved methods of the "elitist exile groups," mainly supporting the American embargo, he has been made an outcast.

What was ironic about the interview was the initial introduction to the piece, as well as the comments from Calzón. The fines and jail time the 70-year-old Gutierrez-Menoyo faced were coming from the United States. Yup, Uncle Sam was seeking to prosecute Gutierrez-Menoyo, for having had the gall to move to Cuba in his effort to bring change.

The interview left me with a plethora of mixed emotions. As a Cuban American, I find beyond belief that the exiled Cuban community's self-anointed "leaders" continue to attack fellow Cubans who seek change in Cuba through a different route than they approve. Why do we continue to criticize and belittle those who seek change in Cuba through dialogue or meetings with Castro just because we do not approve of those methods? The exiled Cuban community should be supportive of all individuals and organizations seeking freedom and independence for the Cuban nation, no matter what track they chose to arrive at the common goal: a *free* Cuba.

As Americans we should be ashamed of our government for continuing to enforce a failed policy, the miserable embargo, a policy ignored by Spain, Mexico, England, most of the other European Union members, China, Japan, and many others. This is a policy that has destroyed many Cuban families through its indirect consequences. A policy that is in place because the US could not stand the fact that Castro thumbed his nose at it as he sided with communism. A policy that seeks to jail a 70-year-old man for being a dissident within a communist nation. The irony is incredible! If, as Americans, we truly desire a free and independent Cuba, then let's tear down the Cuban Berlin Wall. Allow free movement and free trade, and freedom will naturally follow, as happened with Eastern Europe during the Reagan administration. Let's not jail old men, be they misguided or not, for opposing an oppressor from within. Who among the exiled Cuban community, among the "leadership," is ready to do as this man and leave the comforts of the US to take their fight directly to the source of the discontent? Until Cuba is free, we are well served to keep an old adage in mind: The enemy of my enemy is my friend.

XIII

Ricardo and Laura Estella

Laura Estella has always been known as a dynamic woman. Raised in Havana and Matanzas, she easily bounced between the city and her parent's farm with ease and grace. Pictures that have survived the half century since present a woman with a radiant joy, naturally athletic, with bronzed skin and deep, lively, brown eyes. Laura's quick wit and laugh enhance a bubbly personality, one that has survived to this day despite the agonies and hardships of exile.

For Laura, life on the farm revolved around her studies, working for her father in the office, family, riding horses and motorcycles, and taking advantage of the ever present opportunities for fun in an area that boasts some of Cuba's most beautiful beaches. Within a month of finishing high school, she was taking night classes at La Universidad de la Havana, initiating her studies with the goal of obtaining a business degree with a concentration in accounting. Three nights a week she would board the Matanzas-to-Havana "wa-wa" (Cuban colloquial term for public bus), then endure a two-hour ride into the capital, where she would spend another 45 minutes transferring busses, walking through Havana's streets toward the university, stealing a bite to eat along the way, as best she could and crossing the expanses of campus lawns, in order to make her 7 p.m. class on time. At 11 p.m., when class let out, she would spend an hour traveling to the family's apartment in Havana for a quick night's sleep, followed with a "wa-wa" ride back to Matanzas in the early morning hours.

The daily operations of such a large farm were left to her father, Enrique, and his staff of men. Enrique was a pioneer in many aspects, laboring with a blacksmith to create better processes and machinery for cultivating, harvesting and processing hemp into fibers that would become ropes and other products. Enrique's farm was one of the first in Cuba that provided decent housing for all his laborers and their families. Not bunkrooms, huts, or shacks, but true homes, solidly built, the equals to most homes of those days.

Enrique's attributes included a love of country and an unrelenting love of his family: his son, daughters, wife, and extended family. In the years to come, that would expand to include a love for all his grandchildren, a love that occasions the continued celebration of this simple but great man by all that have been blessed in knowing him. He held many virtues desired by mankind — honesty, integrity, courage, and more — and thirsted for knowledge, a desire he labored to bestow upon his grandchildren. When I was a young adult, he would often relate to me the difficulty he had experienced leaving all behind to become a simple clerk at a drive-through convenience store in Miami. Yet he would quickly follow that by asserting it had been worth it, for he and the majority of his family had escaped the grasp of Fidel Castro. Within that assertion he would always find a way to remind me that "freedom is priceless, as is your family. But knowledge is power ... they can take it all away — your lands, your home, your business, but they cannot take your education away. Be sure to obtain your education, no matter how hard it is to do or how long it takes you, because with it you will have the power to guide your own life." It is to him I have dedicated this book, for he, along with my father, is my hero.

At her father's request, instilled by his relentless love of knowledge, Laura began to assist her father with his business while still in high school. Her duties included managing accounts, payroll, and all of those daily office tasks that a successful business must tend to in order to prosper. Her father had asked her, the youngest of three daughters, with only one brother, as she seemed to have a proven knack and the attention to detail needed. Her sisters became accomplished high school teachers, and the brother an agricultural engineer, his potential sadly diminished later in life due to the torments of demons in his mind, a torment that was unable to quell his generous nature and goodwill, a nature inherited from his father.

Laura's first year in college was uneventful, defined by her classes and time spent on work, family, church and her then boyfriend, Ricardo, an architectural student at Santo Tomas de Villanueva University, also in Havana, who was a year ahead of her. Political rumblings of discontent were beginning to resonate throughout Cuba, rumblings that she was well aware of, for these were events discussed nightly at home by her father, mother, and whoever else was present.

"Just think, take note, that my mother, a homemaker," Laura's voice drops as she emphasizes her mother's roots, "a simple woman with minimal education, ... was so in tune to the political process that she would exclaim '¡Este moreno lo odio!' (I hate this brown man!), every time she heard Batista's name mentioned." Laura's voice deepens again, underscoring her mother's fierce hatred. "She was typical of the Cuban women of those days, women who were so well in tune to the daily political machinations that pervaded life. Women who had great hope for their nation and the future it promised, women sick and tired of the lies and abuses of their current political landscape." Laura's hands fly about her, emphasizing her words. "These were women that kept up with [politics] much like their contemporaries in other countries would keep up with their daily soap operas on the radio. Mama was so upset that Batista came and took power with a coup d'etat. She was so disappointed that just months before the scheduled elections Batista had decided that all in power were corrupt, all that followed were corrupt, but that he alone would save the great island nation of Cuba from itself. And perhaps he had good intentions at first, but eventually his own need for power corrupted him too."

Laura's second year in college commenced to a much different political climate than just a year earlier. Recurrent student protests were beginning to have an effect on Batista's regime to the extent that they led to the closing of the University of Havana. Santo Tomas de Villanueva University was spared for a few more years, as it was a private institution whose students appeared to be less intent on political demonstrations, but instead willing to endure hardships as they pursued their degrees. Laura recalls the protests at the University of Havana as becoming more frequent, pushing the limits of tolerance while flirting with violence. For her, the key turning point occurred one day as she was approaching the campus while en route to her class.

My friend Helena and I were headed to class from our friend Teresita's apartment. Teresita in those days lived in an apartment directly across the street from the university, a fourth-floor walkup. Very convenient, and we liked to hang out there while in between classes. On that particular day, a day early in the semester [as] Helena and I were headed to classes, we rounded the corner by the entrance, and all of the sudden shots rang out. We hit the floor — the sidewalk, you know — hard. Shots continued to be fired; we could hear bullets flying all around us. Teresita had stayed

in her apartment, and ... she later recounted how bullets flew everywhere, holes left in her walls. She too had dived for the floor once she
realized what had happened, but curiosity got the best of us and we cautiously raised our heads to see the chief of police, a man whose name I
think was ... Pillar-Garcia. He and his men were rounding up the
protesting students and firing at them. One young man — I remember
him well, he was from my town, lived by my aunt Isabel — this boy
named Jose Antonio Echeverría, he became a Cuban hero. He had been
protesting the political and human rights abuses of the Batista government, and was taken by the police that day, taken about three blocks
away. Teresita was able to see from her apartment as they killed him, shot
him and left him on the street as you'd leave a dog. That was a crime.
That was a good boy, very Catholic, very good family. He became a
national hero. He was killed like a dog, a rabid dog. We used to call him
Manzanita, little apple, for he was slightly overweight, very white, with
rosy cheeks, and — you know us Cubans, we have to give nicknames to
everyone.

Laura is leaning back into her chair at this point. During the description of the shooting she was full of energy, leaning forward, her hands again
flying, as to swat those bullets. Now she is spent, exhausted by the trau-
matic recollections of the day. These are memories that pain her, and with
that pain comes a deep sorrow. This sorrow creases her brow, fills her eyes
with tears. Her pain evident, she continues, lest the memories not become
known, lest we forget the travesties that occurred, the ones that initiated
the path to greatest travesty ever to befall the Cuban people, the travesty
of Fidel Castro.

In Laura's world, the events of that day were a pivotal moment for
many of her contemporary students, as well as for the general population.
The cowardly execution of unarmed students marked the start of a dark
chapter, where the residents of Havana would rise in the morning to find
bodies dumped on the streets. Bodies of those who dared to question the
authority of the day and allowed their guards down; a momentary lapse
of vigilance would be all it would take, and they would become fodder
for the gutters of Havana.

Disgusto, disgusto, disgusto! [Disgust, disgust, disgust!] We would awaken
to see those people dead on the streets, dumped like dogs. People became
so disillusioned, one corrupt government after another, year after year. I

119

don't understand why it seemed as if only the students were protesting. Perhaps that was my reference point. But the Cubans, all of us in general, we were disgusted, disillusioned, but quiet. Only the students protested, but all paid the price. It was a great tragedy, the army was very professional, not political at all, but it was tied up fighting Fidel Castro in the mountains. So the corruption just grew and grew.

Laura Estella left Havana and returned to work full time on the farm with her "Papa," her studies interrupted by growing unrest, to be further interrupted by the revolution descending upon Cuba through Castro. After the fall of Batista, her father's farm was expropriated by Castro's henchmen, following which the family was able to flee to the United States in 1961, arriving in Atlanta with her first-born child in her arms, and her husband Ricardo by her side.

Ricardo had been able to graduate as an architect from Santo Tomas Villanueva before it too had been closed by the government, albeit Castro's government this time. Their last year in Cuba was spent in Havana, Ricardo at work or school, Laura at home with their son, her studies on hold. Their love and commitment to their country continued, made evident by their efforts to assist the resistance movement against Fidel Castro.

In Havana, Ricardo and Laura rented the second floor of a small home that belonged to Ricardo's parents. Laura's sister and her husband rented the first floor when they were visiting in Cuba from the United States. Ricardo's parents, as well as his brother and his family, lived but a few doors away in a similar house. These were typical tropical homes, two stories, an apartment on each floor, dressed in stucco and adorned with a front courtyard and a small backyard. They were located on Calle Norte, "by the Chinese cemetery of Havana, in the Nuevo Vedado neighborhood," explains Ricardo. This home provided them with some relief from the daily frustrations experienced as a result of the increasingly oppressive tactics of Castro against the Cuban populace. It was not that they sought refuge in the home, a safe harbor against the impending hurricane of Fidel Castro. No, the relief they sought, the need to "do something," did not provide refuge, but would have caused their death if discovered and reported by any of the *castristas*. For in their home in Havana, on that quiet street, in the closet of the master bedroom they kept a ham radio transmitter.

Ricardo and Laura Estella

The resistance movement against Castro was comprised of men and women from all walks of Cuban life. And while the organizers were known to most, the rank and file members, such as Ricardo and Laura, had been organized in a cell-like manner as a means to insure some safety. They knew who was immediately above them, who they received instructions from and reported to, they know who were their subordinates, those who they were assigned to manage and direct during those tumultuous times. But never a direct line to the top, never a word or any direct contact beyond the layer above or below. This method would allow the resistance to maintain its activity if a certain cell was found, and limit their losses.

This is why there was a young man who came to their home three or four times a week to work on the radio, a man known as *"el técnico"* (the technician). They did not know his name, where he lived, if he was single, married or a widower. He did not ask of them for anything, not even their names, and they were careful to use generic pet names for each other in his presence, never their true given names. It would be *"querido"* (darling), *"amor"* (love), and *"cariño"* (sweetheart), and the like. The only offering the young couple were ever able to provide to the young technician was the ever-present, ever-brewing Cuban *cafetera*— that potent little cup of Cuban coffee, *el cafecito*.

The technician would arrive quietly on those hot tropical evenings, exchange quick pleasantries, at times accept the offer of Cuban coffee, and then would go to work in the closet of the master bedroom while Ricardo and Laura would draw blinds, turn on the TV, and for all the prying eyes in the neighborhood appear to be a couple sharing a quiet evening at home with a friend in front of the television.

Later in Miami they would confirm their thoughts that the technician was updating the Cuban resistance with what was occurring with the exiles' efforts, such as the preparations of invading forces. He would also provide those exiles outside Cuba with updates as to the preparation for the invasion by the resistance movement in Cuba. Ricardo and Laura knew, as did the rest of the resistance in Cuba, that when the invasion was launched they would be notified so they could initiate their assigned task for that long awaited day. Although there was more than one transmission hub in Havana, let alone Cuba, theirs could have been "the one."

The invasion came. Bay of Pigs (Playa Girón) was chosen at the last moment — according to Laura, "a poor location, a swampy low-lying area, terrible for an invasion, as history has shown. I have read — and some Cubans in the know have claimed — that the change was forced upon the Cuban invaders by their American benefactors."

Within the resistance movement all were notified and dispatched according to previously detailed plans. Ricardo did not go to work, but went with members of his team to their assigned target: to occupy the national radio and television stations located in Santiago and transmit pro-resistance messages, as well as anti-Castro propaganda.

The start of the invasion was self-evident with the bombing of the Cuban Military Airport. In telling of this, Laura Estella pauses, and a long sigh escapes her lips, the defeat of that weekend vivid in her mind, projected onto her face, despair evoked by her body language. She quickly regains her composure, though, and continues detailing her recollections of the events.

> All was cut off due to the bombing. We never saw the technician again, we never saw anyone else of those that we knew were in the resistance movement against Fidel Castro again, with the exception of Luis C., a close friend of ours and an electrical engineer who was the direct boss of the technician.
>
> Initially we were told by the Cuban government that the airport was bombed by a disgruntled Cuban air force pilot, but the reality ... was that he ... came, most likely, from the United States, or perhaps from another country that had been supporting the resistance movement and fighters, such as Guatemala. All day, that day — as there was an ammunition storage depot on that military airport base — all day, we heard and felt — *BOOM! BOOM! BOOM!*—... these explosions. We also heard and saw the planes as they came directly over the house on their approach to bomb Columbia, as the military airport was called. We knew it was the start, and later we knew that it was not just the reported lone, disgruntled pilot that the initial Fidel Castro propagandists told the Cuban people, because that lone man would have had to [have] been something else to fly so many different planes.

Laura Estella's hands become reanimated with the recounting of the bombing raids, flying through the air of her living room in South Florida, evoking the images in her memory of that day. Just as quickly her animation almost completely ceases, as she turns back to her recollections.

"Ay," she sighs again. "But either the attack on the military airport was not enough, or they were held back because they did not destroy all the planes on the ground, and enough planes survived that attack so as to be a decisive force later in the week against the resistance, as well as against the invasion of Bay of Pigs. The invasion ..." And here her voice trails, tears threatening to breach a dam constructed and held for forty-five years. "Ay, that invasion," she whispers, with another sigh. "What a mess. Those poor souls, lost so many of our friends died there, so many true patriots were lost — dead or off to political prisons for torture and slow, miserable deaths."

I ask Laura if we should stop for the evening, and continue at some later date, but she won't hear of that, and insists on continuing, insists that her and Ricardo's story be heard, for they are living history; with the passage of time memory might fail, health might fail, and they do not want their recollections to fail to be known.

"The invasions that came to be known in this country as Bay of Pigs happened in April, and it empowered Fidel Castro, emboldened him, to further implement his restrictions and oppression of the Cuban people. By May of that year he had closed all the Catholic universities and high schools, including the one where Ricardo was just completing his studies. Ricardo was able to finish, barely in time. We were so naive, all those lies told to us, to the exiled Cuban community and to the resistance in Cuba. We were so very naive, we thought we were going to win. We had trusted the United States and what they were telling us. We were rejecting Fidel Castro's propaganda, his slogans, his lies, but we sure swallowed everything the United States told us, how that the first Catholic president of the United States, how he [John F. Kennedy] would surely not permit a communist country in Latin America, less so in the backyard of the United States, a mere 90 miles from Key West. We didn't just believe all that, we were convinced. Ninety miles from US. We really thought that President Kennedy was going to save us — no, no, *perdón*— not save, but provide support, that he and the United States were our friends."

Laura is now reinvigorated, reenergized by a shot of fresh Cuban coffee, as well as by memories of the events that occurred, and strives to explain as much as she can, with Ricardo nodding his assent or occasionally interjecting to clarify a point or expand on another. Ricardo adds, "So, with the Bahía Cochino (Bay of Pigs) invasion, what followed was three horrendous days. Fidel Castro was taking people right and left to the firing squads, then [with] the taking of the [Catholic] universities and high schools, our nervousness — like everyone around us — was increasing daily."

Now Ricardo and Laura relate how there was no more immediate need for a transmitter; if anything it had become a huge liability. Castro and his army had wiped out the resistance. The operating technician had disappeared, along with many friends and acquaintances, and the discovery of the transmitting equipment would bring certain death by firing squad in front of *El Paredón*. No judge, no jury, no appeals.

Ricardo continues to relate his recollection of the events of those days. Calm at first, occasionally his voices rises with emotion, but he always speaks in a dignified manner, with an evident love for his compatriots and homeland. Sadness is etched in the deep furrows of his face, wrinkled with seven decades on earth, four and a half waiting for an embargo to work.

Ricardo does not fit the image of what most Americans assume to be your typical Cuban: light skin, almost pasty white, with deep, piercing blue eyes, topped with a full head of graying hair that was blond in his youth. Many generations have passed since his ancestors came from Spain to Cuba, but he still retains those European looks, as do many Cubans. But when he speaks he is evidently Cuban, given away by a strong accent. Ricardo carries this accent easily, with no thought or concern for it and how it may define him in the eyes of others. This is an accent that seems to accentuate his good looks. Clean-shaven, soft-spoken, a deeply religious man, generous to a fault, with a seemingly unending love and compassion for all members of his and Laura's large family — seven children, twenty grandchildren (with more to come), and even two great-grandchildren, to date — these qualities make him loved by his family, as most men wish to be, but few are ever truly able to enjoy.

He is a daily communicant, with a passion for his faith and the Catholic Church as great as his passion for his family. His personal trinity is completed by his devotion to his profession, his beloved architecture. This is a man who has been called a genius by the likes of Donald Trump, but his true genius is in how he has partnered with Laura Estella to be so successful as parents and faithful as members of the Church.

Ricardo subconsciously scratches at his palms as he continues to speak. It is as if the ink of memories has stained his hands and he vainly tries to rub it away. "The Monday following the invasion of *Bahía Cochino*, instead of going to work, I went to a friend's home. I had a job with a government agency — the government was building a new neighborhood of five- and six-story buildings, a housing project like those you see in New York City, and I had been hired as a project architect before I had even graduated — ... that was allowed in Cuba in those times. But that day I was afraid to go to work. The agents that worked for Fidel Castro in our office could never figure me out, could not tell what my position was until it was evident once we fled Cuba for the United States."

Laura Estella sits up and interjects, "Fidel Castro had his agents going to all the work centers and picking up people, thousands of peoples most of [whom] suffered great barbarities or even lost their lives. A good portion of these simply disappeared."

Nodding in agreement, Ricardo continues, "Most of the employers had sympathizers of Fidel Castro. Most of these were members of the *Comité de la Defensa de la Revolución* (Committee for the Defense of the Revolution, a tactic Fidel Castro used to control each individual neighborhood or village). This was even more so in the governmental offices. These people kept lists of those who were considered 'disaffected,' quite simply, those that dared to utter as little as a complaint or two around the water cooler, a complaint deemed to be against Fidel Castro and his revolution. These people kept lists of those that were disaffected and those who were sympathizers of Fidel Castro."

"*Sí, sí,*" exclaims Laura, "and Ricardo's salvation was that he kept his mouth shut. He was very dedicated to his work as an architect and drafting, and," Laura emphasizes, with an underlying tone of relief, "he kept his mouth shut. Thanks, God!"

"Keep in mind," she continues emphatically, "that the rounded up 'disaffectors' — men, women, youths, elderly, pregnant women, whomever — these were all rounded up by Fidel Castro, taken to a large theater in Havana called "*El Teatro Blanquita,*" as well as to a large sports complex called "*La Ciudad Deportiva*" (The Sports City), a very large facility with track and field areas as well as several baseball diamonds. There they were kept for days and weeks on end in subhuman conditions, as if they were dogs in a kennel waiting to be gassed."

Ricardo and Laura Estella spent the next several days inquiring discreetly for friends. "We would knock on doors to inquire about this person, or that one, and no one would open their doors, no one would talk to us," relates Ricardo.

Laura seems lost in thought for a moment, apparently thinking of the events stored away long ago in the deepest recesses of her memories then suddenly sits up and adds, in a matter of fact tone: "*Miedo. Ellos todos tenían miedo.* (Afraid. They were all afraid.)" She explains that the morning following the Bay of Pigs invasion, when it was evident that it had failed, she had told Ricardo that he should not go to work, that he should go somewhere else for the day. He left with Luis C., while she stayed with her friend, Luis's wife. "We both had newborn babies, and would frequently get together, so we decided it would not seem out of the ordinary if we just stayed together that day. We had made up our minds that if the agents of Fidel Castro came asking for Ricardo or for Luis we would just act dumb and pretend that for all we knew that had left for work that morning. We hoped this would in turn give us time to alert our husbands so they could evade capture somehow. Luckily we didn't have to speak to anyone that day; no one came knocking on our door. Our neighbors on both sides were not as lucky ..." Laura's voice trails off, as tears begin to brim beneath her soft brown eyes. Her chest heaves as she takes a deep breath. Then she waves off my protests, regains her composure once again, and continues her story.

"We saw armed men, Fidel Castro's men, come to the house next door where another architect lived. Little Ricky's nursery had a window that looked over this man's house, and from there we saw them enter, and then heard his little girls screaming, pleading, 'No! No! No! Don't take my daddy away! Please don't take him!' You could hear the man pleading for his life in front of his family; you could hear the agents ransacking one room after another, things thrown, dishes breaking, people crying. What a drama! How horrible it was. My friend and I were just standing there, two young women with their little kids, tears streaming down our faces, afraid to move or make the slightest noise for the fear that we would attract the attention of Fidel Castro's men, and be next. All the while we both struggled, deeply," Laura leans forward to add emphasis, "deeply we struggled with the urge to cry out, to try to rescue that man, his girls, to do anything — something! But we knew that to intervene would have cost us any chance, any hope of surviving this ordeal. It would have cost us our lives, and quite possibly [those] of our families. So we just stood there, unable to stop crying silently, praying for that poor man and his family. We never saw him again. We never knew what happened to him. Soon after that, a few weeks later, the wife and daughters were also taken away by the government men. By Fidel Castro."

Ricardo and Laura Estella continue by recounting friends who disappeared in those days. Laura Estella says one of them was Rogelio González Cortez, a "professional, a good friend of ours." Classmates, friends from the university and from their church also disappeared or were executed: "Juan 'Juani' Periera was a student, a member of the Catholic men's group 'La Agrupación,' as also were Ricardo and Rogelio. Juani was a pacifist, and he was picked up that week and we never heard from him again. They were good people, members of the Catholic Church, members with Ricardo of the *Movimiento de Recuperación Nacional* (Movement for the National Recovery, an anti–Castro resistance group), the 'MRN.' Years later, once we were in the United States, in Atlanta, we found out that he had been held for a few days and then shot to death. He was just a student. On the other hand, with Rogelio, we knew right away, for they didn't even bother to make a pretense of taking him away, they just lined him up with others in front of a wall and killed him."

The week following the failed invasion was full of uncertainties: of their friends, of family, of the future. Going to the homes of friends just added to the increasing nervousness, as the few who did brave their fears enough to answer the door had no answers. Many of the folks they knew had seemingly vanished into the warm, thick, tropical air. "We assumed," Ricardo continues, as Laura blows her nose and wipes her tears away, "that they had gone into hiding, and that we would see them soon again or at least hear from them. But in the end, few were hiding; most had been taken by the men of Fidel Castro and were not hiding but dead. For many we did not know what had happened to them until we arrived in the United States and were able to make inquiries through their families. A fate that we could not have also avoided if they had found the transmitter."

"Ah, yes, the transmitter, what happened to it?," I inquire.

It turns out that the transmitter was wrapped in plastic that evening when Ricardo returned from hiding during the day at his friend's house. Once its gray metal body was tightly bound in its plastic shroud, a hole was dug in the backyard, and all the transmitting equipment interned into the Cuban soil. "As far as I know, it must still be there — Calle Norte numero 7 — waiting, waiting for us to come get it again," says Laura with a quick laugh, Ricardo chuckling in agreement.

Ricardo returned to work the following day, explaining his absence by saying that the bombing raids had knocked out his television set and he was unable to be sure he could go to work, an explanation taken and unquestioned by his bosses, for many others in the Cuban workforce had experienced the same problem. He continued to work diligently, kept his mouth shut, finished his studies and graduated from the university. At the first opportunity available to him, he left with Laura, his son, and other family members to United States. He had seen a large number of friends and neighbors taken by Castro's agents, never to be seen again, had begun to feel the noose slowly tightening around his neck, and was aware that time was running out.

Preparations were made to leave Cuba, as "following the invasions, the collective hysteria and despair of the Cuban people reached proportions that I could have never imagined," explains Laura. As most Cubans, they left with only the clothes on their backs, their memories safely stowed with the hope of a quick return and the power of their knowledge and education in their minds.

"We left everything in the house," says Laura Estella, "when Ricardo and I, with the baby, went to the airport to try to leave, to go to the United States. We knew it would be taken away from us, so we didn't try to take much. We left artwork hanging on the walls, sheets on the beds, clothes in the closet and dresser drawers. We left the food in the fridge and the dishes in the sink."

Trying to leave through the airport proved to be another increasingly stressful event for the couple. They would pack a few clothes, but mostly the items needed by their infant son: bottles, diapers, safety pins and such. They would then go to the airport, to stand in a sea of people vying to reach the ticket counters and purchase seats on departing flights. Then they would go to the departure waiting area, and go through a thorough search by agents of the communist government, only to find that their seats had been sold multiple times and that they were unable to board an airplane to freedom, but would have to return home in despair to the house in Havana.

In order to salvage some hope of seeing their possessions again, Ricardo and Laura Estella had invited a young, newlywed couple to remain at their home, with the agreement that the house was theirs once Ricardo and Laura Estella were able to leave Cuba. After their third attempt to flee the increasingly chaotic island, Laura felt as if she could no longer take the overwhelming stress and decided to stay home with her friends, "while Ricardo went on his own to see if he could get us seats on an airplane out of the country. The plan was that he would go with *Abuelo* Ricardo, his father. If he was successful, *Abuelo* (grandfather) would return to the house for me and the baby. It took Ricardo three tries, but on the third he saw our friends, Helena and Johnny. Johnny had some sort of business ties with the Dutch government and was a friend of the Dutch ambassador to Cuba. Well, on that day they were leaving via a Dutch airliner, along with the Dutch ambassador, and in that manner they secured seats for us also. We had no idea they were leaving that day, and it must have been the hand of God that Ricardo ran into them at the airport amidst all that chaos."

They were able to leave that day for the United States. The only possessions besides their clothes that they were able to bring was a medallion of the Virgin Mary that Ricardo had received when he had initially joined 'La Agrupación,' as well as the bridal veil that Laura Estella had worn on her wedding day. She had taken her coat apart, and sewed the veil into her lining where it was not discovered during the repeated searches at the Jose Marti Airport in Havana. Laura Estella did not have any jewelry to bring, as what little she owned she had entrusted to her sister when that sister left for Miami a year earlier, and such items were not being confiscated at that time.

Having confirmed seats, they were able to advance at the airport beyond the departure lounge to an area called '*La Pecera*' (The Fishbowl). A glass, enclosed area where those who were most likely departing were herded, and no longer allowed to speak with the friends and family who had come to see them off. In this manner Ricardo said his good-byes to his father, uncertain he would ever see him or his mother again. Luckily they would be reunited the following year in Miami.

In this waiting area, Castro's agents would continuously harass their fellow Cubans. This was done with the hope that a person waiting to leave would succumb to the pressure and attempt to strike out physically or verbally against the agents, for which they would be arrested and lose their seats.

Prior to arriving at the airport the first time, Laura Estella and Ricardo had already heard of the abuses, and had a pact that once they reached the fishbowl waiting area, they would quietly endure whatever humiliation or torment was thrust upon them, for they were determined to reach their goal: freedom in the US. Laura says that once they reached the fishbowl, keeping that promise was easier than she had expected, as "by then we had gone through so much, such sorrow, such horrible things, but at that point I had my ticket, I had my seat, and I was getting out, no matter what. What a dramatic event that was for us!"

That was May 19, 1961. On May 1 Fidel Castro had announced to Cuba and the world, despite all his previous denial, that he was a communist, and a Marxist-Leninist at that. The young couple that remained behind in Ricardo's and Laura Estella's house lost that home within a few short months: Castro and his agents took all the homes and removed people as they saw fit. Shortly after that, the couple was able to flee to the US, albeit with just the clothes on their backs.

Two years following their arrival in Atlanta, Ricardo moved his family to Miami after the birth of his second son. The move was made to be closer to friends and relatives, all of whom were waiting for the expected quick fall of Castro, as the US government imposed restrictive measures against Cuba, culminating with the embargo.

"We stayed in Atlanta, Georgia, for couple of years; Ricardo had a good job as an architect that a former classmate had helped him obtain by recommending him for it. But we went to South Florida to be a part of all that was happening, of the activities being organized in preparation [for] the return of us, the exiled community ... to Cuba. As this was during the time of the American involvement in Asia, the Vietnam War, the government of the United States was recruiting heavily from the exiled Cubans, as well. We were told many times, 'First Vietnam, and once we finish cleaning up there we will all go to Cuba.' With that promise we lost even more of our young men. My neighbor's brother, barely 20 years of age, was killed there, as were many more I can think of but try not to. You see where that promise got us, those lies, and we believed them! Like everyone else in Miami and South Florida we had such high hopes. *¡Desengaños!* (Disillusionment!) Once again we were fooled."

Laura Estella appears exhausted; a tired expression hangs about her like a fog. Yet once again when I offer to cease for now, to let her rest until some other time, she dissents and emphatically express as her wish to continue. "For years afterwards," she starts, and then repeats, "For years and years and years I couldn't talk about this. I couldn't talk about Cuba. I was just unable to speak about any of this. I wouldn't think about Cuba. I couldn't even dream about Cuba. I had created a total mental block, for the sadness was too great to bear — it was just too great to bear. I did not have the courage for decades to speak about this, only lately," she says again emphatically. As Ricardo looks upon her quietly, lovingly, nodding his head in agreement, she whispers, ever so softly, "Only now."

"The things that happened must be told. The embargo ... was so hard in Cuba when we were there, and it is now so much harder.... When we were in Cuba we would buy all the baby food we could, for it would only be available briefly, as were the majority of groceries. For weeks, when we arrived in Atlanta, Ricardo would be working and I would go to the supermarket, and for weeks I would cry at the sight of so much food, apples, oranges, meat. Bread! It was overwhelming after having the hardships of trying to find food in Cuba at the beginning of the crisis. The shelves in Cuba were already empty when we left in 1961. Our friends, our families and all other regular Cubans were already suffering. In Cuba we were bombarded daily with propaganda through public loudspeakers: 'We will win! We will win!' And so on. *¡Que jodienda!* What a bother! We were starving but we were going to win? Win what?"

Laura Estella and Ricardo both explain how the members of the Committee for the Defense of the Revolution suddenly were everywhere, almost as if they had exponentially multiplied. These Cubans, fellow nationals, were given by Castro the right to come into any Cuban household, to sit in the living room, in the dining room, among any of the residents or guests, so that they could monitor all conversations and report anything that they deemed subversive to Castro and his government. Following the failure at Bay of Pigs, Laura Estella further explains, members of the *Comité* seemed further emboldened; the suppressive tactics and intimidation increased. The incessant propaganda that had initially been confined to work centers and business districts seemed everywhere, messages blaring from vans affixed with speakers, roaming neighborhoods like ice-cream trucks, calling children and adults to rise against the imperialistic Yankees, to defend the homeland, with an incessant mantra: "We will win! We will win!"

"We would send help as we could to those left behind, but eventually almost my entire family was able to leave Cuba, as was Ricardo's, as well. So after a while we personally did not continue to send money or medicine on a regular basis, but we have friends that still try to, as well as some family, the daughter of my brother, Adriana, who we try to help as we can. But the embargo — hmph, what a farce."

The couple relates how they see the embargo as a failed policy, a policy that is imposed upon the Cuban people with no thought to its consequences. Initially supportive of the embargo, in recent years Ricardo and Laura Estella have come to see it as a failure. "This was supposed to get rid of Fidel Castro, but instead it just hurts the regular people in Cuba. If the United States government wanted to make the embargo work they would enforce it. Instead they keep playing with it, completely unaware or uncaring that they are playing with people's lives. The American embargo did not allow Adriana to come to the United States for her father's funeral, does not allow us to communicate with her on a regular basis, does not allow her to have even a faint semblance of hope for the future. She and those left behind suffer and struggle daily just to get by, while Fidel Castro and the members of his political party live a good life, offering our beautiful beaches and natural elements to tourists from Europe, Canada, Mexico, and elsewhere in exchange for their money."

The hope placed upon the presidency of John F. Kennedy Jr. eventually gave way to despair, to a resignation that the United States, despite all the positive propaganda toward the exiled Cuban community, would neither come to Cubans' rescue nor facilitate of self-rescue. The US would act and react in a manner that was beneficial for the US, regardless if the outcome of those policies would be the further suffering of another nation.

Following the Bay of Pigs invasion, the Castro government's relationship with the US continued to decline, reaching perhaps the lowest point during what is known in the US as "the Cuban Missile Crisis." Castro could still be counted on to make his own rules, as unpredictable as ever, running his economy into the ground, blaming the United States for his economic failures, yet looking for every opportunity to solicit and obtain some measure of relief from the US. Laura Estella explains that during these tense times, emotions within the exiled Cuban community also seemed to hit their lowest point, as hope was being lost for a quick solution to the Cuban crisis.

About two years after the Bay of Pigs, the prisoners, the exiled Cubans caught by Fidel Castro, were exchanged for food and medicine and what have you, things needed by Fidel Castro already, so early in his dictatorship, as he mismanaged the country's economy. By then the consensus among the exiled Cuban community was that President John F. Kennedy had not been a good president, but his brother, Robert Kennedy — there was a man that truly held us and our situation in his heart. Robert Kennedy was so upset over the Bay of Pigs, he truly felt our pain. But who knows what could have happened if he had become president of the United States. The poor soul, he too was shot and killed. What a barbarity.

The presidents that followed John F. Kennedy — with their attitudes toward Cuba and the embargo — served only to first raise, then diminish our hope. They would come to court our votes, raise our hopes, and then — nothing.

The 90 miles between Cuba and the US, more precisely Cuba and Key West, rather than fostering a closeness between the two nations, Laura says,

really worked against the Cuban nation, did not bring us closer together but served to further spread us apart. The United States then enacted *la Ley del Ajuste Cubano,* the Law of the Cuban Adjustment, a measure that we believe came about due to their guilty conscience, a result of first offering help and then removing that help at the last moment in the debacle of the Bay of Pigs invasion.

But then we lost confidence, we lost hope. The exile movement at first was of such a large scale, and of course as we all know by now comprised primarily of the professional class. These weren't the rich, for ... there weren't that many in Cuba. The rich were located in the United States, were from the United States — American citizens and corporations.

This law did help us, the exiled Cuban community. It allowed those that had been in college in Cuba, who had to leave their studies behind ... to continue their courses of studies in the colleges and universities of the United States for free, through grants and mostly through scholarships. I too could have applied to finish my studies here in the United States, but I decided against it at the moment, as I had a growing family, and my husband Ricardo was very busy in his profession as an architect, a business that was growing quite well. Yes, I could have, many did indeed, but I chose not to.

Again Laura appears dejected, shoulders sagging with the weight of her recollections, but still she is insistent in continuing, and waves off my attempts to continue another day, another time. "*No, chico, no te preocupes*; don't worry, I am really fine." She continues to speak about the embargo, refusing to beg off for the evening: "No, look, the fact is that it [Cuba] was all lost, as a consequence of the laws and policies of this nation, of the United States…. The problem of Cuba … that of the exiled Cubans and those remaining on the island, that solution needs to come from us, from the Cubans. Not from the outside, not from other nations, not from the United States. For every time that they would get our hopes up, or allow others to get our hopes up — this was followed with despair, with 'Oh, we caught them with arms hidden, or training in the Everglades,' or any of many other reasons for taking it all away again, including the hope. It was a game, a game upon a game, you know?"

Laura Estella's voice breaks, and floodgates of tears are released. Still her hand waves off my attempt to cease for now, and with a soft voice, full of tender love for her nation, mixed with sourness from the hopelessness of the Cuban situation, she continues:

After all these years you can't help but harden to the situation, to the reality. You read about the people in Cuba, in Miami, on the seas in between, of the sacrifices, Father Varela's life, the quality of the people, the collective intelligence of Cubans, how Havana was compared to Paris — it was called the "Paris of the Americas." Intellectuals, philosophers, liberals, what a society! But then you read about the end of the 1800s, the [Cuban] War of Independence and the manipulation that followed by the United States to try to keep Cuba within their possessions. In the end the United States was unable or unwilling or simply just decided against keeping Cuba, but kept Puerto Rico instead. Why Puerto Rico and not Cuba? I don't know, but they almost did keep Cuba. My heart also breaks for Puerto Rico. There is no reason as to why the United States kept Puerto Rico. Jose Marti, the great Cuban hero, would say that Cuba and Puerto Rico are the two wings of a beautiful bird.

I cannot understand how the United States came to create and force upon us the Platt Amendment. The United States let go of the Philippines, but kept Puerto Rico and meddled in Cuba. Expansion or the desire to expand must have been the motivator that created this history, a history that Fidel Castro is not shy about using to his benefit, as he rallies the Cuban masses against the imperialistic tendencies of the United States.

You see that you live right next to a superpower and you have to be careful. Just like the Finnish next to Russia and the Soviets. You have to be careful or they will swallow you whole. When I speak to recent immigrants to the United States, like my friend Evita and her family, people that suffered greatly just for being Christians, [I learn] how hard they made it for her to go to school, just because she dared to say that she was a Christian. All the hardships she suffered. When I see all that I give thanks to God that I was able to leave, because I don't think that I would [have] been able to survive the hardships.

Evita, a dentist who managed to leave Cuba in 1998 with her husband and twin sons, met Laura Estella through a mutual friend upon arriving in South Florida, and over the subsequent years, despite their age difference, the two exiled women have forged a close friendship. Evita and Laura have shared many Sunday afternoon barbeques under the hot Florida sun, reminiscing about Cuba, faith, and the fate of those left behind to eke out a living under Fidel Castro's policies. Laura recounts how on occasion Evita has described the hardships of being a practicing Christian in a godless society. Part of Castro's scheme to control the Cuban people has involved separating them from their birth families at a young age, so that the youth, the future of the island nation, are shipped off to residential high schools where they are housed in coed dorms where anything is allowed, so long as it does not go against the so-called wisdom of the leaders. Raging hormones and lack of supervision creates demoralizing circumstances for practicing Christians such as Evita. She would hide under her covers on her top bunk, praying for relief, while "*el relajo*," the party, marched on under full steam. Evita was ridiculed for her beliefs, denied entry initially into high school and college, but a single-minded stubbornness saw her through all the trials. Laura recounts,

Evita was determined, yes, that she was going to study, [and go] to school, to college — that she *would* make it. She was ridiculed for her beliefs, for not participating in *el relajo*, and so on. Fidel Castro knows what he is doing to the youth of Cuba — he has created a youth that is rotten to the core. This man, Fidel Castro, has destroyed the Cuban family, he has divided the people to control them and has putrefied their souls instead. The abortion rate in Cuba is so high now, that it is not uncommon to hear of women who have had 20 or more abortions in

135

their lifetimes. There [are] no birth control pills — how could there be when there isn't even aspirin! So the Cuban youth [go] on like animals; they have absolutely no concept of morality. Evita warned me that these stories would be hard to believe, for it is so horrible [for] youth and families in Cuba, but I have heard and seen and know so many like Evita, that I know this is true.

For a committed, lifelong, devout Catholic like Laura Estella, with seven children and numerous grandchildren, the idea of a limited family imposed by a government policy is an unconscionable act, repugnant, a violation of the most basic of human rights. Laura Estella shares the tales of young Cubans she knows, many of whom have not been allowed to have children and have been forced to have abortions or sterilization procedures. The young woman who does manicures at a local storefront shop had two boys while still in Cuba, before she was able to flee, and found herself at the delivery table being sterilized, following the birth of the second son. No questions, no permission, no consent obtained, nothing — "They just did it." This graceful lady continues to mourn her loss to this day, unable to have more kids, unable to have that little girl she so desired. Laura Estella decries these abuses:

> Like the Chinese, [Cubans have] no human rights.... How can that be? How can the world allow this to happen and to continue to happen to this day? All human rights in Cuba are violated daily. These people, like that manicurist, these are the generation raised within the regime, who didn't know any better, and yet they flee when they can. They see that system as total failure, they see it as a total monstrosity. When these stories, the stories of those anonymous people suffering now in Cuba are made known, the world will be....

Laura pauses, her ship drifting off course, blown away by the thoughts and images of abuses in her beloved homeland. Suddenly she perks up:

> Think about it! How Hitler, in all his craziness, and the German people, who are so intelligent, ... arrived at the horrific levels of the monstrosities they committed, and compare that to Fidel Castro against his own people. Hitler raged against the Jews; he was terrible, *de madre*— the worst horrors. Moving the Jewish people, ... from here to there at his whim, and then off to death. But this man, Fidel Castro, doing this ... worse, to *his own people*?

Ricardo and Laura Estella

Exasperated and exhausted, Laura slumps back into her seat, sighing heavily with the weight of her sorrow for her nation. "*¿Que es esto, chico?* What is this, how can it be?"

How could it be that the Cuban people have allowed this to happen? "Those are complicated answers," she allows:

Fidel Castro seized upon opportunities, created many more, and hood-winked an entire nation — no, the world — through his initial propaganda. Well, I suppose you really have to live the system, to be there in Cuba, to know the system. That system by Fidel Castro — I did not live it for decades, but I did live it long enough. To see the suffering elderly, with no food, no supplies, no recourses left, that stays with you forever. In 1959 or 1960, the corner grocer of our block, a Chinese immigrant, lamented that he had left China with the hope and promise of a better life in Cuba, but he told me, "It will all end, it will end soon; you will see, this is just going from bad to worse." I did not want to believe him, but he was right. That system, the communistic system, when it first came about, the pope condemned it, stating that it was "a system intrinsically diabolic," a terrible thing.

Communism is not an economic theory ... communism is a lifestyle, and you are either with them, or — well, I suppose that there are no other options allowed, as long as you wish to breathe and live.

Laura Estella marvels at how the product of this repressive, closed society, the generation that was raised in the so-called "Cuban Paradise," has so readily abandoned all the communist ideals forcefully ingrained in them from an early age:

Jesús, the carpenter that does some work for Ricardo, married, had kids, divorced and remarried, then fled to the United States just a few years ago. A hard worker, willing to work all the extra jobs he can get his hands on so he can go to Cuba every couple of years or so to take clothes, medicine and money to his ex-wife and their children. I know many like him, his age, now in their twenties, thirties and forties, a generation that has fled from Cuba, was raised in that pressure cooker of Fidel Castro's ideology, and they do not want to talk about Cuba, want nothing to do with Cuba. They go back, send monies as they can, only because they have family there that depends on them. Only my generation wants to talk about Cuba. Those that come now, who were raised there and suffered so much ... they have no patriotism toward Cuba, no love of country. They would never speak of Cuba again, if they could. There is such a vacuum in them; having had no Christian education, none, they desire it so much.

We return again to the embargo and the effects she sees, but this is too complicated a topic for Laura Estella to cover simply throughout our conversations. There is this incessant angst in her and others of her generation whom I have had the privilege to speak with over the years. "There is so much left to [do]. I feel bad for the likes of Elpideo and Echenique, that they are aware that they don't have much time left on this earth, that most likely they won't live to see any change happen." Laura harbors no hope for relief from the embargo, and is instead rather distrustful of the intent of the US policies on Cuba. Sipping on that ubiquitous cup of coffee, she states,

the United States Department of State has created a new office called something like the "Peaceful Change in Cuba" office, in order to "be ready" when the change comes. So many of my fellow exiled Cubans have signed up, saying that they might as well at this point, that they might as well sign up with the Americans, 'cause nothing else is working, the embargo has not removed Fidel Castro, and so on. But me — no way! Forgive me for that, but when you read and study Cuba's history in relation to the United States, and you see the [American] efforts that are self-serving at best ... I say, "No thanks.' I agree with Payá, that the solution to the problem of Cuba needs to come from the Cuban people, and that we need to not look outward to see who is going to bring what to this event. How will we accomplish this? I don't know; only God knows, I believe.

We are motivated, ready to do what needs to be done if we are not restrained by self-serving policies and laws. You see it when Father José, for example, a visiting priest from Cuba, a native of my province, Matanzas, comes here and asks if all those in the exiled community who consider themselves to be of that same province would donate just one dollar each to assist in the repairs of churches in Cuba. "Sign me up," I said, as did all those I told and the ones [he asked]. Quickly, no questions asked, we are ready to help when we can, where we can. When you see that reaction of those folks, my generation, ready to help, it gives you hope. This is a generation that was disillusioned with the church in Cuba for not fighting against Fidel Castro, for not intervening in the politics.

But the church should not enter into politics. The church *is not there* to make politics, and these folks have come around to realize that, and gladly give as they can to help the church in Cuba. This giving is done in a manner that is not hindered by the American embargo, and we know that 100% of the money goes to the churches.

So many of the initial wave of exiled Cubans are now retired, their children grown and gone, and have such a great drive to help out as they can, for this will be a part of their legacy when they are gone. They are well aware that life is running out, the waters of the pool of life running more shallow every day. Projects such as the one dollar per person for the church are seen as a way to give back to their birth nation, the land they love, the Cuba they miss and desire to be free. The University of Miami has been gathering a collection of the writings and other important documents of exiled Cubans significant for their dedication to the cause and hope of seeing a free Cuba one day. This includes Elpideo, Echenique, and many others. What a gift to us and our children, for we are the future of Cuba and should know the history of her people, at home as well as in exile, so we can keep from repeating it in the future.

How *does* this embargo affect Laura Estella and Ricardo? It affects their hearts, minds and souls. They suffer for its impact on the younger generation, for "the damage it is doing to the Cuban people, those lacking basic needs and human rights on the island, those here in exile that work their fingers to the bone to provide for two families, the one they have here, and the one back in Cuba that they must support or they know will perish in a slow, miserable death. They work so hard to send back clothes, money, medicines. But ... all [we] can do is watch and suffer over it."

Ricardo and Laura Estella say that they will continue to wait, hopeful for the future, hopeful that the "situation in Cuba will change for the better soon." And although hope has matured into disillusionment, they both fervently state that they will always keep waiting. For Ricardo and Laura, a couple that left Cuba as vibrant twenty-something, now approaching the start of their seventh decade, it has been a long wait. Forty-five years and still counting, yet they will continue to wait.

XIV

Jovenes (The Younger Generation)

CARLOS OYARCE

Carlos Oyarce is a young man in his mid-thirties, with dark hair, brown eyes and white skin. "Doesn't quite have the typical Cuban looks," was one of my first thoughts when I met him, "but then, neither do I." Turns out that Carlos is an adopted Cuban, as he was born in Chile, but spent a great portion of his life in Cuba. Carlos and I met at La Peña, and have maintained contact since, mostly by e-mail.

Having lived in Cuba for years allowed Carlos to become very familiar with the system and its oppression of the Cuban people. Currently Carlos lives in Miami, and is involved in the opposition to Fidel Castro, his regime, and their evil ways. He is a principal and a writer for the Web site Fundacionpatrialibre.org, dedicated to exposing Castro's crimes to the world. This Web site has some excellent links to other groups and sites, one of which is a photo comparison of "the Two Cubas," what is seen by tourists, and the realities behind the scenes.

Over time we have discussed, in particular, the treatment of dissidents in Cuba, as Carlos has electronically forwarded to me many letters that originated from the dungeons that Castro has reserved for political prisoners in Cuba. Carlos is quick to condemn the horrible treatment these brave men and women suffer at the hands of the Cuban government. The early 2003 firing squad deaths of three Cubans by Fidel Castro's militia brought decisive words from Carlos. "Truthfully, it is disagreeable to speak about such atrocities, but what better commentary can be given than that found in the international press as it protested these crimes, and is every day more supportive of the Cuban opposition."

The release in June 2004 of a small group of what Carlos terms "*oppositionistas*," mainly called dissidents in the American press, was cause for some celebration, but Carlos cautions that the few individuals released should not lend to the expectation that the repressive and inhuman Cuban jails will soon release its thousands of political prisoners. He does, however, note that these releases resulted mostly from strong and decisive international political pressure. There still remain many opposition members incarcerated, most of these without charges or any sort of judicial recourse provided to them, usually for years at a time. Carlos theorizes that these dissidents were released because the Cuban government is looking to soften its image with the international community. Other events, such as meetings between Fidel Castro's son and the wives of dissidents, inside the embassy of Portugal, are also seen by Carlos as being no more than posturing by the Cuban government in an attempt to defray further criticism.

Carlos points out that "from all these events we can conclude that we are not as weak as some believe, and that the opposition in Cuba is firm, despite repeated efforts to pistol-whip, intimidate, and minimize [the opposition]. The truth of the matter is that [the Cuban government] fears them and sees in them an immense danger." He further proposes that this fear of the dissidents by Castro and his gang will continue to increase as these dissidents acquire further support from the global community, particularly democratic countries.

Carlos thinks recent events in Cuba are signs of an approaching demise of Castro and his regime, the way seismographers see small shock waves with increasing frequency prior to earthquakes. These events include those of the night of February 12, 2004, when a group of *oppositionistas* threw bottles and rocks at the home of the major of state security in the town of San José de las Lajas, near Havana. These are unprecedented events in Cuba, and — although on a very small scale — challenge the authority of the regime, as they test the waters for future events. Carlos also notes the increased frequency of incarceration of *oppositionistas* and the tightening of Internet access, as attempts to control the increasingly discontented populace.

Carlos sees the end for Castro rapidly approaching, in spite of the embargo and not because of it. Carlos also believes that the continued violations of human rights, in particular those targeting political dissidents and their families, is what in the end will galvanize the international community to come to the rescue of Cuba and facilitate in some way the means needed by Cubans to gain political freedom. So sure is Carlos of the imminent demise of Castro's repressive regime, that in his newsletter of June

15, 2004, he states "the time of the end for Castro and his accomplices has arrived, all know this, more or less in months, as it is a matter of marking the days on the calendar. The final events are being released [so that] at some moment you and I will be morally obligated to go the extra mile. It is your turn to renew and ratify your [promise to] the more than eleven million of Cubans that should no longer wait for their freedom, as with all of us united we can defeat this dictatorship. We must put the theory to practice, so that tomorrow, when all this is history, you can sleep soundly with a clear [conscience] and you can look at your sons with your head held high."

Once again, all of us, Cubans — exiled or not, Cuban-Americans, or simply friends of Cuba, need to hear the call announcing that the time is now to set aside our differences and approach in a unified fashion the problem of Cuba as a Cuban problem that must be resolved by us and through us. The misguided interventions of other countries and institutions need not apply.

ALBERTO PEREZ

Alberto Perez can perhaps embody the typical first-generation Cuban-American living in Miami. Born and raised in Miami, he has traveled for pleasure, as well as for commerce, throughout Latin America, and is married to a wonderful Hispanic wife, Maria Inés. Alberto has the direct gaze and self-assured manner of a successful businessman and is fiercely devoted to his family: his recently widowed mother, his brothers, his dearly departed father, and his centenarian grandmother. For Cubans, family is very important, as exemplified by men and women such as Alberto and Maria. Alberto is not only bilingual, he is truly bicultural, as most of us first-generation Americans tend to be.

Alberto recently traveled to Cuba in an effort to satisfy what had been a growing desire to see the land of our elders, "*la tierra de los viejos,*" as he states with a mischievous smile just lurking beneath the surface of his face. This is said with hinted humor, as the true meaning of his desire to visit Cuba is implied: a need to connect to his roots — our roots — by actually touching the earth, breathing the air, feeling the breezes of a land that has been at once foreign, as well as familiar throughout his life.

XV

Las Monjas (The Nuns)

As with most of Latin America, Cuba's history has been strongly influenced by the work of men and women of faith. Catholic nuns in Cuba had a long history prior to Fidel Castro's revolution, following which most of them were expelled from the country, perhaps because they were a strong reminder of his Catholic upbringing.

Laura Estella relates how *las monjas* (the nuns) of her school in Cardenas also had a large school facility in Havana:

> This was a beautiful campus, located in a neighborhood called *El Cerro* (The Ridge). Once I was married and had moved to Havana with my husband, I would go visit them frequently. Most of these nuns I knew from my schooling in Cardenas where they had taught many Cuban girls, including myself. In particular I would frequently visit the nun that had been my teacher in the fourth grade.
>
> Once Fidel Castro took control of the country, he immediately expelled a large number of religious men and women, and some he even did worse. These poor nuns were so scared; they were horrified. For example, this nun would say to me: "Ay, Laurita ..." — she would call me and cry on the phone, she was so scared.... For her this fear was very real. The agents of Fidel Castro had entered forcibly into the house where she lived with some other sisters. And took some of the sisters away, allowed some, including her, to stay under very restrictive conditions. The terror she suffered that day! For her it was history repeating itself, a history she had already lived years earlier under Franco in Spain, when her monastery had gone through the same ordeal, where they came to the house and arrested the nuns. They did not find her because she hid under the house — in the basement, I think was what she had told me. They took all of her sisters away, killing seven of them.... Later on the pope would canonize all seven of them. The others too suffered greatly, including being made to watch as some of their students were taken and placed in front of a wall and shot, right before their eyes. *¡Fusilaron a niñitas!*

Little girls were shot! She was so certain that her fate was inescapable this time; that her time had come and it was going to be a horrific end. For she was unable to escape the images in her heart and mind of the abuses suffered in what was then a not-too-distant past, in Spain.

So I would tell her: "No, Sister, don't be afraid, the United States is helping us, we are in the right and we will win." Hmph! Me, so young and *guapita* (brave), I was so certain of that, so certain the United States would not let us down. *Ay, mijo, que desengaño, que pena.*

So Sister eventually ended up in Havana, in a residential building on the campus of their school. Fidel Castro took all their facilities, all the classrooms, the gym, everything, and these few remaining nuns he kept under house arrest with a female military agent guarding over them all the time. This agent was … their warden and they weren't allowed to leave the immediate grounds around the house. She was unable to sleep, for she had never had a 'guest' like that before, and it unnerved her greatly.

So either very bravely, or more likely very naively, I would go visit them … often in my car, a little Italian Fiat I had then. We used that car to remove and take and hide many of their religious and educational items. I would take whatever they gave me; we would fill the trunk up to almost bursting each time, and then I would take these to where they instructed me to. Usually to private residences where we would hide them in attics and basements for safeguarding. Remember, we were convinced that these injustices by Fidel Castro would not last long.

Laura Estella pauses, sipping from her coffee, her brown eyes reflective of the memories of so long ago, of the disillusionment long since entrenched. "But when the Bay of Pigs exploded…." Her voice trails off, wandering after the thoughts of those days of forty-five years ago. "If I had been caught — just imagine — but you lose your fear, for you are so willing to try to help, so wanting to try to help. Anything, anything: you try to do what you can to correct some of the injustices you are seeing and living, to try to ward off — if possible — … those injustices that are coming toward you and the people and land you so dearly love. And all this while I was pregnant with my first child."

"Sister would need to go to town, to try to procure food, to do her errands. These were nuns that wore a habit all the way to the ground. *Hasta el suelo — te imaginas?* She was a Cuban nun, the principal of the parochial school before Fidel Castro removed her. To not ever wear her habit was beyond comprehension for her."

Las Monjas *(The Nuns)*

Laura Estella recounts how the nun was mortified that she would have to wear 'civilian' clothes rather than her religious order's habits. Despite the sweltering heat, the nuns wore these every day, from the moment they awakened and rose, to when they retired for the evening. When Laura took Sister to town in regular clothes, without her habit for the first time, Sister cried all the way there and back. But Castro was expelling all religious from Cuba. Unlike Franco he apparently did not kill any of them, but he would not let them wear their frocks, or their habits, or — for the men — not even the collars. To do so would mean immediate arrest and expulsion from Cuba, even for Cuban citizens, born and raised in there. Castro had no qualms sending Cuban religious people to exile.

"I understand," Laura continues, after pausing to wipe tears and regain her composure, "I can understand to some point if Fidel Castro had taken offense with the religious men and women that were from other countries, as many were — particularly from Spain. I could see where they would be asked to leave Cuba and return to their countries. But Fidel Castro went beyond that, he expelled Cubans from their own land, against their wishes, because they had heeded a religious calling to serve God. The foreigners — what can you say? But Cubans! Even the auxiliary bishop, the president of the Catholic University, Monsignor Eduardo Boza mas Fidal, and the current Monsignor in Miami, Monsignor Romero, who was but a young parish priest at that time in Matanzas. *El descalabajo complete de una nacion, incredible!"*

These brave men and women had a good idea of the hardships that were to come, yet they labored to stay in Cuba so that they could safeguard their churches, their monasteries and seminaries. They expended a lot of effort attempting to stay in Cuba so that they could fulfill the perceived obligations of their religious missions: to safeguard the spiritual well-being of a nation under assault. These people were glad to be there, desired greatly to be there, even when it was obvious that all would be lost. To expel them from Cuba was for Fidel Castro a means to deny the existence of God, to deny reality, and to create his own reality.

XVI

Politics: The Impact of the Helms-Burton Act

What has been come to be known unofficially as the Helms-Burton Act is legislation that was enacted by the US Congress in 1996 as H.R. 927, titled the *Cuban Liberty and Democratic Solidarity (LIBERTAD) Act of 1996*. The purpose of the act, in essence, was to further impose sanctions against Cuba, as a result of events current at that time, as well as to strengthen the sanctions already in place. In addition to numerous United Nations resolutions, as well as various international treaties, the Helms-Burton Act sought to further enforce requirements delineated by such US laws as the Cuban Democracy Act of 1992, the Foreign Assistance Act of 1961, and an amendment to this 1961 law, titled the Freedom Support Act.

In the weeks just prior to the dramatic birth of the Helms-Burton Act, Congress was debating *lifting* restrictions against Cuba, as a humanitarian gesture, as the fragile economic health of Cuba, following almost five years without support from the Soviet Union, became more apparent the act itself acknowledges this precipitous economic decline, in the opening statement of Section 2 (Section 1 being the Table of Contents), titled "FINDINGS." This section reads in part as follows, as taken from the Library of Congress Web site (http://thomas.loc.gov/cgi-bin/query/z?c104:H.R.927.ENR:):

"The Congress makes the following findings:

(1) The economy of Cuba has experienced a decline of at least 60 percent in the last 5 years as a result of—

(A) the end of its subsidization by the former Soviet Union of between 5 billion and 6 billion dollars annually;

(B) 36 years of communist tyranny and economic mismanagement by the Castro government;

(C) the extreme decline in trade between Cuba and the countries of the former Soviet bloc; and

(D) the stated policy of the Russian Government and the countries of the former Soviet bloc to conduct economic relations with Cuba on strictly commercial terms.

(2) At the same time, the welfare and health of the Cuban people have substantially deteriorated as a result of this economic decline and the refusal of the Castro regime to permit free and fair democratic elections in Cuba.

(3) The Castro regime has made it abundantly clear that it will not engage in any substantive political reforms that would lead to democracy, a market economy, or an economic recovery."

I encourage you to take the time to go online and read these acts in their entirety, a very enlightening process indeed.

Through this act, from its opening lines, the Congress of the United States declared that the economy of Cuba at that time was in shambles, that the Cuban people were suffering as a result of it, and that Fidel Castro was not only the cause of these hardships, but was also entrenched in a manner that would assure the continued suffering of the people of Cuba. Taken out of context with the events of those days, the history of the contentious relationship between the US and Cuba, and the attitude toward Cuba in general at that time, it would appear that this opening volley could just as well have been made as part of a persuasive argument for the lifting of sanctions, the easing of the "substantially deteriorated" welfare and health of the Cuban people. This had appeared to be the direction that the Congress was headed in the weeks just prior to the introduction of this bill. But the easing of sanctions was discussed in Congress, and dutifully reported through the media, Fidel Castro must have taken notice and must have been concerned, for a softening of sanctions would impact his regime in a way counter to his plans and desires. Therefore, as was reported at the time, he instructed the Cuban Air Force to shoot down an unarmed surveillance plane over international waters. The plane was carrying Americans, was an aircraft licensed and registered in the US, and flown as part of a humanitarian mission by a group known as Brothers to the Rescue. The group is comprised mostly of Cuban exiles, and patrols the waters of the Florida straits looking for fleeing Cuban refugees on makeshift rafts. These rafts may carry them to freedom or just as easily to their deaths, as indicated by the number of empty rafts found, and documented in stories of survivors whose raft-mates failed to hang on in rough seas, who drowned and became fodder for sharks.

Naturally, the uproar caused by the downing of this private aircraft, along with the loss of lives was heard all the way to Congress, which, in typical, reactive fashion introduces, passed, and finally approved the Helms-Burton Act (LIBERTAD), H.R. 927, in record time. Quickly forgotten were the speeches and proclamations of the previous weeks in which the misery and suffering of the Cuban people was being upheld as a reason why the American embargo need to be dismantled, or, at a minimum, readjusted in some form. Now Congress was laser-focused on punishing Castro for his flagrant disregard of international law and the sanctity of human lives.

In the immediate aftermath, as well as the months and years to come following the passage of the Helms-Burton Act, it has been evident that Congress played into Castro's manipulative tactics. Castro was able to further solidify his position through more of his fiery rhetoric, rallying crowds of Cubans into a nationalistic frenzy, citing the Helms-Burton Act as further proof of the imperialist, interventionist attitudes and desires of the US. Castro sold to the Cuban people that the one and only item on the US agenda for Cuba was complete and total domination. He further named the coming years *La Época Especial* (The Special Times), a time calling for further sacrifices from the Cuban people. Castro called for Cubans to stand vigilant against a forthcoming invasion by the United States, an invasion that would not liberate them from their hardships, but would instead enslave them to the United States.

This was no more and no less than the typical pack of lies that Castro had been serving us for thirty-six years, and that continue today. It served Castro well: The Cuban people, in fear of the US, rallied around their nationalistic sentiments, fearing an invasion of Cuba, and endured further hardships, suffering, and misery. As a direct result of the deft manipulation of Congress by a despot seeking nothing more than the continued iron-fisted rule of Cuba, and enabling himself and his inner circle to profit and live a life of luxury, Castro's subjects wallow in hopeless turmoil, essentially abandoned and incarcerated, with little to no resources, other than an incredible will to live and an attitude of *hay que resolver* (we have to resolve, we have to make do).

Section 3 of the act, titled "PURPOSES," does not mention fostering fervent Cuban nationalism as a goal, but instead reads in its entirety:

"The purposes of this Act are —

(1) to assist the Cuban people in regaining their freedom and prosperity, as well as in joining the community of democratic countries that are flourishing in the Western Hemisphere;

(2) to strengthen international sanctions against the Castro government;

(3) to provide for the continued national security of the United States in the face of continuing threats from the Castro government of terrorism, theft of property from United States nationals by the Castro government, and the political manipulation by the Castro government of the desire of Cubans to escape that results in mass migration to the United States;

(4) to encourage the holding of free and fair democratic elections in Cuba, conducted under the supervision of internationally recognized observers;

(5) to provide a policy framework for United States support to the Cuban people in response to the formation of a transition government or a democratically elected government in Cuba; and

(6) to protect United States nationals against confiscatory takings and the wrongful trafficking in property confiscated by the Castro regime."

In ten years from the inception of the Helms-Burton Act till now, it does not appear that there has been much success in achieving these declared goals.

Item 1 of section 3 declares the honorable intent of the US government "to assist the Cuban people" to become, essentially, a free and prosperous society, productive members of the Caribbean community. The further strengthening of sanctions does not appear to have fostered the desired prosperity of Cuba, nor has it provided a vehicle through which to gain political freedoms necessary to achieve a democratic society. As proposed throughout this book, what it has done is further entrench Fidel Castro and his control over Cuba. The people of Cuba are much worse off today than they have ever been, yet there is no other future on the horizon for them because the embargo does not foster the dynamic undercurrents that need to occur in order for change to happen. Instead, it stifles them, slowly asphyxiating the Cuban people in an attempt to bring down Castro.

The second item declares to rally the international community behind the American embargo as a means to dethrone Castro. This is where there is much debate within the exiled community. Many of the exiled Cubans I have spoken with will privately admit that the embargo is a failure, simply for the lack of support that the international community has provided for it. The major trading partners of the United States, some that are significant allies — such as England, Canada, Mexico, and the rest of the European Union — all conduct a brisk trade with Cuba, in clear, flagrant disregard of the embargo. These actions necessitate the suspension of Title III of the Act by the US president every six months. No matter which party has occupied the White House or controlled Congress, neither has been able to rally the international support needed to effectively enforce the provisions of the embargo. What if the United States rallied the international community behind this embargo, much like the recent economic embargo of Haiti, or the successful total embargo of the apartheid South African government throughout the eighties. That embargo culminated with the establishment of a democracy, with fair elections open to all races. That was an embargo that the great majority of the international community supported and strived to enforce, adjusting sanctions as needed, in order to deny the apartheid government the benefits of any loopholes it sought to exploit. The most significant factor that led to the successful implementation of this embargo against an entrenched government was the totality with which all nations joined it, evident in numerous resolutions issued by the United Nations. This is the exact ingredient lacking in the American embargo of Cuba.

The third item declares how the United States is concerned about its properties in Cuba, the effect of terrorist plotting by Cuba toward the United States, and the manipulation by Fidel Castro of the Cuban people, where, at his whim, he can control a floodgate of refugees that can in a matter of days, if not hours, flood the shores of the United States, creating a disaster upon the affected Gulf states, notably Florida, overwhelming the capacity of local, state and federal agencies to effectively manage the onslaught. Many lives are placed at stake in these poker games, such as those lost during the last mass exodus, the Mariel boatlift of the summer of 1980. This is a legitimate concern for the United States, but it also speaks of the crises in Cuba, the hardships, misery, and lack of hope, wealth or health within her shores.

The terrorist plotting by Castro appears to be limited to blackmailing the United States as he can, with the threat of unleashing another flood of refugees at a moment's notice. In the weeks prior to the commencement of saber rattling toward Iraq by the George W. Bush administration, the administration floated a trial balloon declaring that Castro had biological weapons with the possible intent of terrorizing the United States. It was a fleeting item in the national media, laughable, showing the lengths to which the administration will go to appear to be doing something in the "War on Terror." Never mind effectively finishing the campaign in Afghanistan. Never mind the hijackers of September 11 who came from our "ally," Saudi Arabia, prior home of Osama bin Laden. Never mind focusing on the capture of our public enemy number one. Instead the administration felt compelled to increase the breath and depth of its campaign against terror by suggesting that Cuba posed a serious threat to the United States. This proposal apparently died a quick death, leading to the selection of Iraq for further action in the "War on Terror," despite faulty "intelligence." This intelligence now seems to have been made up as the administration needed it, rather than based on facts and findings on the ground. In a way, I lament that the Bush administration did not pursue the premise of Cuba poised to attack the United States at any moment with weapons of biological terror. Perhaps this pursuit would at least have led to the removal of Fidel Castro, much like Saddam Hussein was ousted. In invading Cuba, the infighting would have been but a fraction of what has occurred in Iraq, and the loss of American lives would have been negligible, if any, much like the events that occurred when President Reagan ordered the US military to invade Grenada.

The Helms–Burton Act enumerates various military actions by the United States, as well as other sanctions brought against rogue nations with success. In particular it mentions the actions against Haiti, highlighting that these were sought through and sanctioned by the United Nations, which the United States has been unsuccessful in doing against Cuba.

The goal to encourage free and fair elections under international observers, as stated in item four of this third section, is a goal that deserves success. But again, without the international community's support of an embargo, this will not occur, as evident by the continued passage of years with no signs of valid, free and fair elections being held in Cuba.

Item five is probably of concern within the Cuban population, for it reeks of past interventionist activity by the United States. That the transitional government in Iraq was beset with problems from day one does not help. But more so, the history of the United States toward Cuba, as enshrined in the now-defunct Platt Amendment, is something that the Castro regime labors continuously and efficiently to keep in the forefront of the Cuban psyche, ready to be recalled whenever the words "United States" and "transitional government" are strung together.

The last item is perhaps the most political, as it intends to appease the exiled Cuban population, residing within the United States, in particular those who have become naturalized citizens of this country. It seeks to provide these Cubans in particular, as well as other Americans who have had their assets and properties expropriated by Castro, with recourse to obtain compensation for their losses. My family, which had lived in Cuba for many generations, proud of our heritage, lost a lot of assets — property, homes, and other material items — to Castro, and the pain and suffering of these losses was coupled with the loss of our country. But what can we hope to gain through a law like this? The adage that "you can't squeeze blood out of a turnip" comes to mind. In addition, what good would monetary compensation be when our families, friends, and compatriots continue to suffer? How do you put a price tag on that? Rather than seeking financial compensation now through the courts of a foreign country, we should be seeking the return of democracy to Cuba, and then seek redress through her courts, on her terms, with a true jury of our peers. This portion of the Helms-Burton Act has further divided the Cuban communities. Those left to suffer in Cuba state that they have been left to *comerse el cable* — eat the wire. Those left behind have had to endure the hardships of a bleak daily life under the oppressive manipulations of Castro, while the rest of us in exile within the United States have been blessed with a life of relative luxury and comfort. This portion of the act has been interpreted among those in Cuba to mean that exiled Cubans are plotting to return to take what little is left. For the exiled community this has also fostered a split, in which those who had assets in Cuba are seen as wanting to return to a life pre-Castro, without paying any dues, by those who had to come to the United States or to other countries in order to build some, if any, measure of wealth. It can be seen as the classic crevasse between blue-collar and white-collared communities.

Other portions of the Helms-Burton Act bear discussion. Here are items 27 and 28 of section 2, the "FINDINGS" section.

(27) The Cuban people deserve to be assisted in a decisive manner to end the tyranny that has oppressed them for 36 years, and the continued failure to do so constitutes ethically improper conduct by the international community.

(28) For the past 36 years, the Cuban Government has posed and continues to pose a national security threat to the United States.

Given the date these words were written, we need to update "36 years" to "47 years." Item 27 again attempts to address the international community, this time by trying to shame them into action. But from a Cuban point of view this includes the United States, and the stigma of engaging in "ethically improper conduct" must be applied to the American government, as well. To continue a policy that the Helms–Burton Act admits has failed to remove Castro for 36 years is unethical and improper. The American embargo expired many years ago when the Kennedy administration dealt a murderous blow to the brave souls launched upon Bay of Pigs in 1961, and while secretly negotiating with Cuba and the Soviet Union during the missile crisis in October 1962. At that point a message was sent to the world that, in one way or another, the United States would compromise its principles, even if it meant the removal of its own backbone, causing the death of many men, as long as the agenda included items favorable to the interests of the United States, the Cuban exiles be damned if their interests didn't happen to fall within those parameters. And yet we wonder why the world does not support the embargo.

At the time of the writing of the Helms–Burton Act, Fidel Castro had maintained his excruciating control over Cuba for 36 years. In the 28th item of section 2, the act declares that the national security interests of the United States had been at risk during that time due to Castro's regime. Yet item 1 of this same section states that the Cuban economy is on the brink of collapse, having declined at least 60 percent over five years. How can it be that a country with such an anemic, faltering economy, with a laughable military, and no longer receiving any support, economic or military, from the former Soviet Union, could pose a threat to the United States? The United States just flexing its military pinky could wipe the slate clean in Cuba. It was done in Grenada, Haiti, Iraq, and countless other military endeavors. Could the issue be a lack of courage? A hidden agenda, as some of the exiled leadership has alluded to? What purpose does it serve the United States, with a record of military responses toward countries that fail to appease it, to portray itself as intimidated by Fidel Castro? Granted, there are no vast reserves of oil under Cuban soil or waters, and its mineral resources are slight, so there is no economic incentive for the United States to have a democratic Cuba at its back door. Apparently the humanitarian generosity which this great nation has shown in the past does not seem apply to Cuba, save for those already here as exiles or naturalized citizens, the few lucky enough to touch U.S. soil and escape Fidel Castro's nightmare.

Under section 306 of Title III of the Helms-Burton Act, the president of the United States can effectively suspend the initiation of portions of the act that directly seek remedy by United States nationals against the Cuban government for the loss of property. The president, upon proper notice to Congress, can suspend these portions of the act for six months at a time. During the time that the suspension is in effect, aggrieved individuals or entities cannot bring suit against Castro's regime. Since the passage and signing of the act in 1996, every president has suspended these portions of the act. The act further allows Cuban exiles and U.S. citizens to recover properties from people and entities from any country, that have been allowed by Fidel Castro to develop, maintain, and use them, as indicated under Title IV of the act. But since this includes all of the major trading partners of the United States, the president is placed in the position of either suspending those portions of the act, or essentially isolating the US from its trading partners, as these partners would be denied entry into the country, and their assets frozen and subject to confiscation as a means of providing remedy to individuals and entities seeking justice under provisions of the act.

The Helms-Burton Act does include many provisions that are just and fair, or at a minimum, well-intentioned toward Cuba and her citizens. It provides for the continued support of television and radio transmission to Cuba in an effort to provide Cubans with a truthful counterpoint to views emanating from Castro. Unfortunately, the current administration of George W. Bush has cut funding for these programs, and is quietly seeking to eliminate them altogether.

The act provides for a road map delineating how a transitional government could move into place and then assist the election of a permanent government. The drawbacks of this have been mentioned above.

The act details the aforementioned attacks on three private aircrafts by two Cuban Air Force jets, over international waters in 1996. That section within the Act, section 116, further provides evidence of the continued human rights abuses by Castro and his regime, and concludes with the following three items:

> (b) STATEMENTS BY THE CONGRESS- (1) The Congress strongly condemns the act of terrorism by the Castro regime in shooting down the Brothers to the Rescue aircraft on February 24, 1996.
> (2) The Congress extends its condolences to the families of Pablo Morales, Carlos Costa, Mario de la Pena, and Armando Alejandre, the victims of the attack.
> (3) The Congress urges the President to seek, in the International Court of Justice, indictment for this act of terrorism by Fidel Castro.

As of today, the International Court of Justice has not been capable of bringing Castro to trial.

The Helms-Burton Act tries to cover a lot of ground. It addresses concerns about the Jaragua Nuclear Plant near Cienfuegos, Cuba. The construction of this plant, at the time of the writing of the act, had been halted since 1992, following the evaporation of critical funds and support from the Soviet Union. The act further notes that inspections had raised serious concerns about the quality of construction materials and methods, leading to concerns about the safety of the plant. Images of the nuclear disaster ten years earlier at Chernobyl must have abounded in the minds of the authors, and rightly so. The act brings to light several factors in arguing against reinitiation of construction of this plant, but most of these not as serious as the implied threat of a repeat Chernobyl disaster, with a nuclear fallout that would certainly reach vast numbers of US citizens in the Gulf Coast states and beyond.

Section 113 seeks the extradition of "all persons residing in Cuba who are sought by the United States Department of Justice for crimes committed in the United States." This has been interpreted as seeking the return of the US citizen Robert Vesco to face charges for embezzling millions of dollars in the United States, although it does not mention his name.

The act addresses the exchange of news bureaus, the reinstitution of family remittances and travel to Cuba, the assistance that the United States will provide to the Cuban people, restrictions of Cuban products, restrictions toward financial assistance for projects within Cuba, and many more just as varied issues. The common point between most of those items is that the president is either provided with the opportunity to suspend a portion of the act for up to six months at a time, or that it will only go into effect once the government of Fidel Castro has been removed from office.

The Helms-Burton Act attempted to provide teeth to the embargo, while allowing the logical suspension of key portions to avoid hurting the United States, but the act has served to carry out the agenda of Castro despite its intentions.

Time and again the act calls, directly or indirectly, for the removal of Fidel Castro and his regime as a key condition for the lifting of sanctions, or for allowing assistance to be provided to the Cuban people. This is a great idea, one that all of us within the exiled Cuban community, natu-ralized Americans of Cuban decent, and the majority of American citi-zens desire. But the Act's one glaring omission is that nowhere within it are means stipulated to directly provide full, adequate, and unencumbered support to achieve this goal.

The US government needs to take a long, hard look at this act, as well as other enacted policies toward Cuba, and come to the realization that the current plan of course has failed, in portions and collectively since the current administration has a tendency to "stay the course, come hell or high water," as demonstrated in Iraq and elsewhere, the much-needed changes that would either modify the embargo to placate concerns of the international community and thus bring it onboard, or that would elim-inate the embargo for another course of action, are changes that will likely continue to elude us, thereby further postponing democracy in Cuba.

XVII

Larry

"I just want one elected official to tell me ... just why is it that my well-earned money, my tax dollars, are being spent to support a failed policy, a policy that failed years, decades ago? Is there someone, anyone, in this administration that can honestly answer that question?" The man with the soft southern accent, tall, with a graying shock of hair and thick mustache, is upset, does not understand the reasoning behind the efforts and money that the US government places behind the efforts to prop up the embargo of Cuba. Throughout our conversations this is a question that resurfaces. Larry Hamlin is a retired gentleman who has traveled to Cuba "more than once" for mostly humanitarian reasons. His initial trip to Cuba, many years ago, occurred after the prompting of a friend, a colleague who baited him with the promise of "a taste of adventure" and the opportunity to see new horizons. That trip lead to others, all organized to help alleviate the medical shortages in Cuba, in particular the shortages suffered by a hospital in Havana that specialized in pediatric oncology.

I had heard a lot about Larry Hamlin for several years, through Norman West of Cullowhee Methodist Church in Cullowhee, North Carolina. In recent years Norman and his church, supported by Larry and his relief organization, had organized a collection of medical supplies under the banner "Crutches for Cuban Children." These efforts had netted two commercial containers full of medical supplies for donation to the pediatric cancer hospital in Havana. Larry's friendship with Norman dates back to their days as college freshmen at Western Carolina University and through the gracious efforts of Norman I was finally able to meet and interview this generous man.

When I first call Larry to introduce myself, he seems to hold back, selectively answering my inquiries until I mention Cuba and my friendship with Norman. Once we breach that threshold, Larry is enthusiastic in speaking about Cuba, his love for the isle and her people obvious. Later

157

we sit at the Cullowhee Café, a diner that has been remodeled in such a manner as to retain the southern charm of its initial proprietors. Larry confesses having enjoyed many meals at the initial establishment during his college years, and takes obvious pleasure in seeing the original owner's children still running the business in such an efficient manner. The familiar atmosphere appears to relax Larry as we speak, joined occasionally by Norman, who occasionally interrupts our conversations with greetings to fellow diners.

Before Larry delves into the reasons that Cuba has so ingrained herself within him, he questions me to ascertain my motives, as well as to determine the depth of my knowledge of Cuba, in particular of the events that lead to Fidel Castro assuming control. As we eat, and pause occasionally to chat with the waitress or with Norman, Larry asks how Cubans interviewed for this book have responded to my queries, and offers suggestions for further people to contact.

"You," Larry exclaims, "as a Cuban American, a citizen of the United States, a person with Cuban blood coursing through your veins, you have a right to demand from your government an explanation as to why it continues to fund a policy that is not working." Larry states time and again that he has yet to meet any federal elected official ("and I have met many!") who can answer this question in a manner that makes sense and is not enshrouded in political obfuscation.

As we converse on the subject of Cuba and the embargo, Larry takes notes, and refers back to them in order to make sure that questions he has for me are asked, that points he wishes to emphasize are made.

"Perhaps, that is a result of the lack of leadership within the Cuban-American and the exiled Cuban community," I offer. "Nope," he quickly replies, "it is not a *lack* of leadership, but a leadership that has self-serving goals which do not truly include normalization of relations with Cuba. These leaders all have agendas of their own, agendas that appear to be well served by the continuation of the embargo, agendas that do not hold the benefit of *all* Cubans at heart."

Larry is concerned that the possibility of a civil war in Cuba following the death of Castro comes from the narrow-mindedness of the leadership of the exiled community in Miami, fueled by the hostile atmosphere of Miami's radio talk shows. "There is no sense, no justice in telling someone who has lived in a particular house in Cuba that he will have to give up all ... that he owns so that someone in exile can return to what they abandoned almost 50 years ago." I am the son and grandson of some who did leave behind so much in Cuba, who fled with many hopes and fears, praying for a quick return, only to have the ensuing years squelch any vestige of hope. I know that all of my grandfather's assets were nationalized and exchanged for worthless stock, stock for which there was never any accompanying payment, as was promised. Is there no recourse for my grandparents' heirs? My parents and grandparents did not want to flee, but were forced to, as the threat of losing their lives hung heavily over them daily in Castro's Cuba. I believe they have a right to claim what they left behind, as this was an exodus forced upon them. The argument that my family was in the United Sates living well while those who occupied their homes have led a life of misery does hold a fair amount of truth to it, but my family did not ask to leave, they worked courageously hard against Fidel Castro once he divulged his Marxist-Leninist ideals, only to have their hopes dashed with the debacle at the Bay of Pigs invasion.

Larry is able to understand and empathize with this argument, allowing that "the details will be for the courts in Cuba to address in the future, but the focus needs to be on the big picture now, on the removal of Fidel Castro from power. It dismays me that Fidel Castro remains in power, and he and the top five percent benefit and prosper while the rest of the island nation suffers."

Coffee cups are refilled, dishes removed, and our conversation continues in stride. "It is of particular interest to me, as a student of Cuba, to know that the complete historical picture is presented, Larry says.

"I think it would be interesting ... to go back to the beginning and present the relationship between Fidel Castro's government and the United States government, and — Larry arches his eyebrows to quietly emphasize his following points —"take a fair look at what happened following the revolution. All of this information is well documented, as well as available, as to when Fidel Castro came to the United States, came with his hat in his hands ..." Larry fades, shifts, takes a sip of coffee and then, as if reinvigorated by the juice of the bean, continues: "Fidel Castro came to the United States, in the opinion of a lot of people, to make a partnership with the United States government. He was looking for support."

I interject that it appears to me that Castro was seeking the highest bidder in an effort to see who would best fund his quest to remain in. Larry agrees and continues:

"Fidel Castro came to the United States and was told that he was a piece of shit, a pimple on our ass."

The president would not only not see him, but was busy playing golf in Augusta, Georgia ... [so] he had fifteen minutes of time to spend with Vice-President Nixon, and "you better make it quick and be humble." And so the United States government sent Fidel Castro back to Havana, Cuba, with his tail between his legs, his pride heavily wounded.

My way of thinking, and forty-five years of proof, says that was the wrong way to treat him. So, Fidel Castro came shopping for the highest bidder, and all we did was insult him. Fidel was not interested in anyone other than the United States primarily, followed by the Soviets; the Chinese, who had yet to develop as any sort of world power at that time, he dismissed. But the Soviets jumped at the opportunity to be at the United States' back door, and Fidel Castro played that offer well.

Larry takes pains to make sure that he is not being interpreted as an apologist for Castro, or worse yet, as a supporter. He seeks to be seen as a concerned citizen who is deeply dissatisfied with the policies toward Cuba, in particular with the Embargo. Larry admits that he is "emotionally involved with Cuba," yet he is proud to be an US citizen, one who has sought the truth of the intentions of the United States toward Cuba, only to be met with reactions ranging from stonewalling to dismissiveness from our elected officials.

The government in place before Castro, Batista's government, was corrupt, a thinly-veiled, propped-up puppet regime in place by the US government and organized crime to facilitate their agendas. Having a playground for the mob provided a way to decrease some of the violence in Chicago and New York, at the very least moving that south to Cuba. Larry says that the US government turned a blind eye, "you do this, we do that," as a means of having a common ground to be able to approach and deal with organized crime.

But then Fidel Castro seized upon this to validate his claims of corruption — Fidel Castro was good at his PR; he initially presented himself as the great Catholic savior, yet less than five years later he was agnostic and seized all churches in Cuba. I believe that Fidel Castro has a demented mind; he risked his life on numerous occasions for what he believed in and saw many of his friends killed. That takes a toll. But within all that, Fidel Castro was determined not to allow the United States government to once again control Cuba.

As the waitress refills our coffee cups, Larry pauses, apparently lost in thought for a moment or two. Then he bobs his head toward Norman. "Norman can also tell you this from his visits to Cuba, that there is one thing instilled in every Cuban's mind and that is, first on their list, that they don't know what to do about Castro. He's got them." Softly he repeats this, as Norman nods his assent:

He's got them.... *La Barba* [The Beard]. They fear him, wish him gone, but to a man [they] are committed to being a sovereign nation.

The embargo, nobody could really explain it — it was bullshit when it was initiated, a plan to starve Castro out. It should not have been something that could be supported by any rational mind. It's proven itself to be ineffective ever since. Now, there are all sorts of people that will tell you that the embargo is a partnership between the United States government and the Fidel Castro government, because it is the only thing that enables Castro to remain in power. You can't rise up when you are trying to feed your family.

I do know this: the United States government has a presence in Cuba beyond the Special Interest Section. There is a working relationship with the security forces of the United States and the security forces of Cuba. And it's a ... very opposite to adversarial, very cooperative ... but who knows ... somebody — well, as I said before, the devil is in the details.

Larry appears flustered, as if he wishes to say more, but is unsure of the impact or implications of what he's just said. But he recovers:

The fact is that the United States does not publish their imperialistic tendencies, yet note that our foreign policies have not changed dramatically in fifty years. They [the US government] want to colonize Cuba, unwilling to say they want to make it into the next Puerto Rico, but that is in the game plan. They [the US government] have a 1200-page booklet on "How to convert Cuba after Castro's passing." It just doesn't put in the last few words — *convert Cuba to what?*

Here's the real joke about the whole embargo: You think that there aren't Pepsi Colas available in Cuba? Or Marlboro cigarettes? Or Nike tennis shoes? Or Chrysler automobiles? The only thing that prohibits the distribution of [those products] in Cuba is that Castro has an economic stranglehold on the country — they can't afford to buy a pack of Marlboro cigarettes, but they'd love to. They'd love to have Nike tennis shoes.

In his travels throughout Cuba, Larry has noticed the resourcefulness of the Cuban people. Unable to buy Guess t-shirts, they set up counterfeit shops to produce replicas, a trend seen with many products, most of these — if not all — bearing logos of US products. In the markets are apples from North Carolina and Washington.

"The economic aid to Cuba from the United States was about $800 million a year and is now over 1 billion dollars annually," Larry continues. "You are not talking about a country of two hundred and fifty million people, but you are talking about *eleven* million spending 800 million dollars. Cash dollars — not credit dollars … cash dollars to buy this stuff."

Our discussion gravitates to how Cuba has served the United States very well as a bogeyman of sorts, in order to facilitate the continued funding of unnecessary military hardware and to advancing the personal and political agendas of a few at the expense of the majority, how Cuba has not been allowed to clean its own house.

"That's not going to happen without U.S. intervention — that's just not how this country works," states Larry. To which I respond: "Well, that *is* an issue for this country, the United States, to work out. That is not a Cuban issue. Why can't we be allowed to work out our own problems? The exiled Cuban community has been prepared and willing to sacrifice themselves, to train, to go into Cuba in order to topple Fidel Castro and bring change to Cuba, but the United States government has not allowed it as part of the missile crisis agreement."

The issues are complex. Larry says he doesn't want to "talk about my own little frustrations about Cuba," but could perhaps put me in touch with important folks in Washington and elsewhere. I remind him that this book is not an in-depth sociopolitical study, but rather an attempt to demonstrate the impact the embargo has had on the average person in Cuba and in the United States. Larry sips his coffee quietly, contemplating this position, and then continues. "What I can tell you: my own personal opinions and frustrations over seeing people that I care about — or love — suffer because of some kind of bullshit, imperialistic, non-performing, *non-performing,* policy. I wish I understood why the embargo."

Our conversation on this foggy morning in North Carolina turns to how—when Larry initially traveled to Cuba—fog lifted to reveal a gorgeous "Carolina Blue" sky, without a single cloud marring its vastness. Larry reveals that it was through a peripheral family connection that he had the opportunity to first visit Cuba, a trip that when proposed appealed to his sense of adventure and so therefore he quickly signed on.

Larry did not anticipate the depth of the adventure, nor the length, "spending the next eight years of my life hustling medicines and crutches" over several trips to the island nation. As to the potential impact of his goodwill, Larry states, "I don't know that I have done a bit of good. I don't know that the stuff I have taken did not end up in the [Cuban] government's hands—I know for a fact some of it did. But all that aside, I wish that someone from the United States government that forms our foreign policies could sit down with me ... and just explain to me what the United States government ... [is doing, and] why? For a policy in place for forty-some years, there has got to be an explanation, 'Yeah we are achieving this, yeah, Castro is on the ropes, yeah....'" Larry's voice trails off. "But there is none of that.... Nobody can explain it."

The trial balloons that President George W. Bush sent up prior to the invasion of Iraq occupy our conversation as the waitress refills our cups. Following the invasion of Afghanistan, in the weeks prior to the invasion of Iraq, Bush administration officials stated that they believed Cuba has a "biological warfare research and development effort" and that this was a potential threat to US Security. Larry states that he remembers this vividly: "I was in Cuba at the time, and they, the Cubans, were all scared that they were the next target of the Bush administration."

As recounted by Larry, this apparent attempt to test the will of the citizens of the United States for an invasion of Cuba "then fell by the wayside," as "people in this country said 'Are you nuts?' Next thing you know we are at war in Iraq—but that is a different story."

> But Cuba did come up on the radar screen—I was there—and Cuba was on high military alert. They [the Cubans] were pulling these 1950-something MIG airplanes from where they hide them on the Road to Pinar del Rio. Forget the fact that they don't have any jet fuel or rockets, they were pulling them out.
>
> The Cuban people, one thing they do believe in, they believe that Fidel Castro beat the United States in a war, as they consider the Bay of Pigs invasion a war, not a failed invasion, and for that they hold him up

as a hero. I tried to explain to people — I was hanging out with doctors and really smart folks, and Cubans are really smart, even if jaded. Yet no matter how smart you are, if all the information you get is unilateral b.s. from the state-owned television, after a while you are going to believe it. Well, the thought, the response [in Cuba] to the Bush administration was, "Well, if the United States invades us again, we will beat them again."

With the beginning of a grin softening his face, accompanied by a soft chuckle, Larry continues: "First of all, I can't see any reason that the United States would ever want to invade Cuba, other than [that] the guy in the White House is a belligerent, cowboy maniac. I cannot explain any of his policies; I can't explain how he got elected — other [than] that I voted for him in 2000."

"If there ever was a declaration of war against Cuba ... it would be a touch of a button and [Cuba] would be eradicated. Forget about Bay of Pigs, about life rafts and canoes and commandos and soldiers. It would not be done that way."

The tangent of this discussion leads us to conclude that a war with Cuba would produce results not unlike the initial war with Iraq, the Desert Storm war, with its infamous and sobering "Road to Baghdad" scenes of total annihilation of the Iraqi soldiers by the US military.

A door bell welcomes a flux of customers into the café. Southern accents abound as we turn again to discuss what may motivate Castro.

For Larry it is important to ask that people in this country take a good, hard look at the events that led to Castro declaring his country a Marxist-Leninist paradise. "Look at the historical developments. Fidel Castro is not a communist; he is clearly a whore selling himself to whoever has the money. It is all about Fidel Castro! He was looking to see who would support him. Every family [in Cuba and abroad] has been touched by Castro."

Once again I feel compelled to ask Larry how he became so committed to helping Cuba. Where does the "emotional attachment" that he speaks about originate? Larry says that his best friend, starting in the third or fourth grade, was a Cuban-American boy. The close relationship between Larry and Tony's family became further cemented when Larry lost his father as a young teenager.

Larry

I became pretty much a regular member of their household. His [Tony's] grandparents and mother were from Cuba. I was very close to them. I just spent a whole lot of time in the throes of the revolution, how beautiful the country is, how Papa Torres was smuggled out of the country — it was all very intriguing to a kid. We had actually planned to go to Cuba when I was ... eleven? No, twelve — 1958 — and then the revolution took place.

Instead of going there, Mama and Papa Torres fled here. Then I went on, school, college here, career. I had an opportunity, just out of the clear blue sky in 1995. I guy I knew asked: "Want to have an adventure?" I'm always up for an adventure. "Well this is a *real* adventure!," he replied. That initial exchange developed into a trip from Atlanta to the Bahamas, and on to Cuba, supporting a journalist.

In spite of all his research, the experiences of his youth, numerous conversations with other previous travelers, supplemented by readings, and topped with all he had heard over the years, Larry was unprepared for his initial experience of Cuba. The shock of experiencing Havana for the first time was striking to him. "I can't describe it to you. you need to see it for yourself, but it is like ..." Words fail him here, and he stops to gather his thoughts, then continues: "The shock is palpable when you walk out the airport door. From there, the ying and yang of the ..." Larry is still struggling to find the right words, to paint the appropriate picture so he can share with me the shock of that moment.

The variances of what once was obviously a very beautiful, very highly advanced society. Havana at one point in time had to be one of the most beautiful cities in the world. You can still see that, still see the ghost of that, but it is all falling apart. It is not uncommon at all for someone to go to sleep down there at night and die during the night because the ceiling caved in on them. They don't have any other choice. They can't fix it. Yes, they are doing a pretty good job with band aids and bubble gum and whatever else they can steal or barter, but....

Larry's voice fades. "It is very intriguing to me. The family thing only grew gradually. When I first went there, my first trip, I stayed in Havana. I met some people in the neighborhood where I was staying in the *Casa de Escobar*. It broke my heart. I love kids, and kids [were] following me around." Larry emulates a child's high-pitched voice: "'Are you an American?' It is very unfair to most of them. [I] didn't know what to say because of ... the embargo." Larry's slow southern cadence diminishes to a near standstill for a moment.

Then he's going full steam ahead again: "The Embargo is more than economic: it is also people, and you need to know that! They [the US government] intentionally separate the people so they don't know us and we don't know them. The only voice that we [have] got is these highly opinionated people in South Florida, who sometimes ... through their initiatives, step overboard and do more harm than good. They are flexing their political muscle, that lobbying muscle they have. I cannot see that it has ever helped the [Cuban] people, although ... I do recognize the fact that money and articles from the Cuban-American community ... are the biggest economic engine in Cuba."

The good fortune of Cubans who have relatives in the United States, versus those who don't, was a painful, stark contrast to Larry while on the island. Yet for all the suffering and hardships around him, Larry knew that he would return to Cuba. The only portion of Larry's relationship with Cuba that he will not discuss is the exact number of visits he has made there. He does not want to make that information public, although it is obvious that he has traveled to Cuba many times. "Too much. I don't want to publicize any numbers." Larry notes, "Some agency of the United States government is aware of every American that travels to Cuba. This is done, certainly more strenuously after September 11 because the systems are more in place. I can also tell you, as a matter of fact, that the Cuban government knew my whereabouts and activities every day I was on that island. When I was taking small duffels of medicines and medical supplies, it was not a problem. When I started sending three containers, 40-foot containers, it became a problem. Because, again, it is all about politics and power and perception."

Larry holds that at that point he was no longer welcome to continue his humanitarian missions in Cuba since it had become a statement to Cubans that help was being provided by foreigners because Fidel Castro did not care in the least about their welfare. While out on the street, one day in Cuba, a pair of government agents stopped him, dismissed his hired interpreter and escorted him to see the deputy minister of the interior, who controls all of the armed forces in Cuba.

The fact that these were plainclothes agents raised alarms within Larry, as "in Cuba ... the ones you have to fear are not the ones in uniforms. The ones you have to fear are dressed just like you are. It was a man and a woman, very nice, very courteous."

Larry

The interpreter was dismissed with a curt hand gesture and warning to not be seen with Larry again. Larry was addressed in Spanish as well as English, informing him that the Cuban government was well aware of who he was and what his activities in Cuba had been, and expressed appreciation for his goodwill, but told him he "would not be doing that anymore." Larry was further prohibited from seeing again those to whom he had brought medical and economic help, the doctors, nurses, patients, church people and others who had endeared themselves to him and occupied a special place in his heart. He would not be allowed to visit "his kids" in the hospital.

Larry recollects those events in a soft voice, but then erupts:

> And I for damn sure would not be allowed to [go with] groups of people like I did [with] Norman to visit the hospitals that I had supported: the Children's Cancer Center in Havana, in Varadero, and the miraculous facility called *La Casa Llena*, which is the home for — the campus for — people in Cuba that suffer Down's Syndrome. When we were there, we opened the sign-in book only to see Jimmy Carter's signature. What they have done is miraculous, and I have been able to help them in terms of dance equipment and things they need, musical instruments that they need for their programs.

The Cuban government official not only told Larry that he wouldn't be going there again, but that if he did bring or send any more supplies in the future, the government would be taking them. Larry was well aware that the policies and laws stated by the US Department of Commerce made it clear that humanitarian supplies provided to Cubans could "only be received and distributed by the ultimate end-user, an NGO, a Non-Governmental Organization."

> To compound the matter, they [Cuban agents] took this rather innocuous Jewish guy, who is a friend of mine — he is harmless, he is the meekest — well, he is married to a Cuban woman and has done a lot of good. Between us we have sent bicycles, wheel chairs, crutches, a lot of things, in addition to just plain ol' medical supplies. He went [to Cuba] last September, checked into his house where he stays with friends ... [and next thing he knew, agents] put him in the back seat of a Ladas, and took him somewhere into the basement of a house, into a cell and left him there for eleven days. They ... never told him a thing. Never an interview [and he] never saw anybody from the [United States'] Special Inter-

est Section or the Cuban government. On the eleventh day they took him to the airport and made him buy a ticket. They told him not to come back.

Upon his return to the United States, and following a period to regroup, as well as to calm his shattered nerves, Larry's friend contacted the Cuban Embassy in Washington, D.C., and essentially asked "What happened?" He was informed that the charges against him in Cuba were for providing monetary support to dissidents, distributing cash to dissenters. This is a charge that infuriates Larry, as he explains, "Rich would never do that. I would be more inclined to do something like that than this guy would. But over there — in the past we have taken money to support churches, a number of churches. Particularly I have worked with the Cuba Council of Churches, which again, is controlled by the government."

Larry is unapologetic for his role in assisting churches and individuals in Cuba. "We were able to get money into the hands of individual churches, individual people who needed it; and if that is supporting the Castro regime — so be it. We helped — I took artificial breasts to a fifteen-year-old girl who just had a double mastectomy. If that is supporting the Cuban government, then I plead guilty."

Again Larry returns to his central premise that the US government owes its citizens, in particular to members of the Cuban-American and exiled Cuban communities, an explanation of the embargo. If Larry were writing this book, he says that he would make the central question that of "trying to find [a way] out of— at the best — a very questionable foreign policy."

Larry advances that "if this [is] in fact a democratic society, then why in the hell can't somebody explain why this failed policy — by any definition —*failed* government policy has been in place for forty-five years. I don't think you will get an answer to that because there is some complication that we don't see. But then, what are the ulterior motives? I have been on the ground; you are a Cuban American — we should know better than some idiot in the State Department. We should particularly know, as this has been in place through — I can't even tell you how many — ten presidents? Why did Jimmy Carter keep it in place? Bill Clinton was in favor of relaxing it, and was about to, until the Brothers to the Rescue [were] shot down."

We return to discussing Larry's donations to Cuba and I ask him where his donations come from. He receives substantial donations throughout the Southeast, including South Florida. Some people from the Cuban-American community in that area who provided donations to Larry and his organization requested that their identities remain anonymous for fear of repercussions from the exiled Cuban community. "I have buddies in Florida who help me; they send toys to Cuba but they don't want anyone to know they are doing it. That is why they give it to me. It's phenomenal."

Larry has inquired of his friends in South Florida as to the secrecy, for which he has received responses that are mostly the same, which he says are typically along the lines of, "Well, you don't live down here; you don't understand the pressure that still prevails." We discuss this typical incongruity of Cuban-American families: how they appear to be intent at punishing Fidel Castro at all costs, yet they are concerned about their family and friends left behind, a concern reflected in the generous nature of their *envios*, sending to Cuba as much as they can, through whatever means are available. This is counterproductive to the goals of the embargo, goals that claim to punish Castro.

"The only way to punish Fidel Castro is to remove him from the position of power. You are not going to punish him by starving to death the population, and there are a lot of people that will say that to you." Larry reclines into his seat. We have driven back from the café to Norman's offices to finish today's dialogue, following which there appears to be a golf date at hand.

"I will go on record as saying this: the embargo empowers Fidel Castro. It is just common sense, and I have observed it from being on the ground. It empowers him." Larry pounds the table where we are seated. "Not only does it give him absolute control, but it gives him the platform to get up and say 'You know why you have no beans? You know why you live like dogs? Because of the imperialists to the north. Because of *El Bloqueo*.' And that allows him to rail, and rail, and rail on."

Two of Larry's golf companions check in, say their hellos and depart to the café for their breakfast, after a bit of good-humored ribbing exchanged by all present. We return to the topic at hand, and Larry marvels as to how the Cuban people have given in to Castro, but immediately counters that opinion. "You [have] got to remember that this guy [Castro] is the only voice in town." We note how with the absolute control of all media he has "brainwashed a lot of people. Yet this country has given him a lot of reasons to do that." Larry, lowering his voice, wonders if there may be a covert relationship between the two governments, as the embargo appears to be crafted in a manner that solidifies Castro's death grasp on power.

> People in Cuba, rich and poor alike, believe that Fidel Castro sold them a bill of goods. Initially the revolution was a seemingly good cause and wildly popular. Shortly thereafter he took them down the wrong street. Everything was pretty rosy in Cuba during the years of the Soviet Union tossing five to seven billion dollars annually into an island that size. That is a lot of cash infused. When it stopped, the suffering started. The people realize that the revolution doesn't work. That philosophy doesn't work. Some have suffered, but if you are Fidel Castro's buddy, you want for nothing. And there are a couple hundred thousand of them. The rank and file of Cuba has been through the pits. As long as he is there, as long as there is no hope in sight, he's got them and they know it. They know it because of the CDR [Comité de la Defensa de la Revolución] and the absolute military control.

Larry leans forward, firing questions at me, emphasizing each by slapping the table. "So what is the deal? Why is the United States government reluctant to discuss the embargo with United States citizens? What is their justification? How does it penalize? How does it punish Fidel Castro? How does it weaken the Castro government? Does it not empower? ... Those are the questions that need to be answered."

XVIII

Loss of a Cuban Hero

Here in the mountains of western North Carolina, the leaves are changing colors. Soon winter will be upon us, trumpeting the end of the year, the end of a cycle. On a day like today, the leaves are a poignant reminder that we, as mortal humans, must also leave our branches, falling onto the earth so that others may follow.

Fleeing an oppressive regime for the promise of comfort and prosperity in a country such as the United States is a goal many Cubans aspire to obtain, yet few reach. The majority who have obtained this goal arrived in the 1960s. Among these were men like Joaquin Casajuana. Joaquin was a great man, a dear friend of my family, a man who I grew up around — not just him, but his family. His daughters were my babysitters. His son, a friend, is someone I admire greatly. Joaquin has been like an uncle to me. He came to the United States from Cuba in an effort to provide a better life for his family, as the option of remaining in Cuba under the dictatorship of Castro had no appeal to him.

Like most of his generation who fled to the United States, Joaquin has gone on to his just rewards in heaven without the opportunity to satisfy the longing in his heart, that burning desire to return to Cuba. Like many of his compatriots, he was a graduate of that toughest of all schools: Leaving Homeland. This is a school with coursework requiring a trek across the Florida Straits, a trip toward the hope of a better life. Most, if not all, of those men and women who have fled hope to one day return to a free Cuba. Most also see that dream of a return stay beyond their grasp, as the toll of time and disease arrives to take them to their heavenly rest. These men and women are our everyday heroes of Cuba. They labored for the good of family in a strange and foreign land, they kept alive the hope of a return to their beloved homeland, and they had the forethought to instill in their sons and daughters a love for the old country, for Cuba.

Among these men and women there are some of such high caliber that they demand special recognition. Some of them have been profiled in this book. One in particular, with his passing on, September 23, 2006, deserves that special recognition, for he is truly the embodiment of a Cuban hero.

Cuba has lost a champion of her cause on this day. A man whose ever-consuming goal was the education of those he came in contact with so that they might see Cuba and her issues in as clear of a light as he had. C. Elpidio Perez was surrounded by his family, visited frequently by friends in his last days; he died at home, in his modest apartment in the heart of the exiled Cuban community in Miami. I can count myself as a lucky one, one of the few who had the pleasure to know Elpidio and talk with him. We chatted on the phone and in person, and exchanged written materials. Some of our discussions were apparent fodder for the column Elpidio wrote for *Libertad,* a small, Spanish-language, independent monthly newspaper distributed in the Miami area. The following is brief synopsis of some of those conversations.

GUANTÁNAMO

Following the US invasion of Afghanistan, Elpidio held that the United States had converted a familiar name for all Cubans, Guantánamo, into one of notoriety, through use of the Guantánamo base as a concentration camp for captured prisoners. Prior to that distinction, Guantánamo was a holding area for Cuban rafters during a massive wave of emigration initiated by Castro, a wave that the United States was determined to repel, as these were unwanted people. Even further back, the Guantánamo base resonated in the psyche of Americans and Cubans alike as a place where Haitian refugees were taken, prior to their return to Haiti.

For Elpidio the real question was "what is Guantánamo?" He held that it is a piece of Cuba, of the national Cuban territories, upon which there is a US naval base, a fact recognized — if not accepted — by Cubans. As Guantánamo is one of Cuba's deepest and widest bays, it is easy to see how it would attract the interest of a naval force. At the end of the nineteenth century there was an American club, the Club of Long Beach, that held frequent events there.

Following the Spanish-American war, the United States recognized that Cuba had a right to independence. Yet with the Platt Amendment inserted into the Cuban constitution, the United States muscled their way onto Guantánamo to protect its interests. Several treaties between Cuba and the United States failed to return Guantánamo to Cuba, culminating in an unilateral directive from the United States in 1934 that Cuba would receive a yearly sum of two thousand dollars, payable in gold, as "rent" for use of the land that the bay occupied, as well as direct payment to Cuban landowners whose properties were appropriated. The final agreement held that the United States would *only* use this land for a naval base or for the production of coal, necessary for the steam frigates of the time.

Elpidio would discuss all these treaties and conventions in great detail, both with me, as well as in his column. He held that the agreement between the United States and Cuba for the lease of Guantánamo and its terms, while forced, had been agreed upon by both nations. Therefore, the United States had grossly violated these terms when it started using the base as a detention center, and more recently as a concentration camp.

THE FIGHT AGAINST FIDEL CASTRO AND FOR CUBA

Elpidio could converse for hours about the state of the fight for Cuba, for the removal of Castro and the return of democracy to the island. He found the state of current affairs for Cubans, both on the island and in the disorganized exiles, as lamentable and sorry. For Elpidio, the Cuban people were held in a vacuum, without direction or leadership, sick and tired of seeing the continuous loss of precious time and effort. The self-serving political interests of the exiled leadership, he argued, were leading to a great disillusionment and, placing Cubans in a pathetic situation.

In March 2002, Elpidio lamented the so-called leadership of the exiled Cuban community, a group that seems incapable of transcendence, of constituting a true front of legitimate opposition. Fidel can bask in the luxury of knowing that there is no exiled Cuban force he needs to fear; he holds the exiled Cuban community as mere puppets of the administration currently occupying the White House.

Elpidio strongly voiced disgust at the current state of the exiled community, a community paralyzed by the fear of attempting to accomplish goals that were not in the best interest of the United States. He vigorously questioned how it could be that the well-being and liberty of Cuba was dependent on the interests of a foreign government. He pointedly asked how it could be that the fight for one's nation, the rescue of her institutions and needed political change could depend on a Congress and president of a foreign country. The fight for Cuba, while not a lost cause, is a patient on life support. There is no Cuban in exile who refuses the above intrusions but those who submit cannot truly be Cubans. Elpidio called on each and every Cuban to labor for the freedom of Cuba from Castro's tyrannical grasp. He called, again and again, for Cubans to remember the principles of their country's founders, that they come together collectively for the common cause of Castro's defeat.

THE CUBAN NATION

Perhaps reflecting Elpidio's thirst for knowledge, coupled with his education as an attorney, a student of all laws, he would converse for extended periods on the legitimacy of the current communist constitution. Not surprising, he held it as an invalid article, another lightly-veiled ploy by Castro in his need for controlling the nation. Elpidio was capable of reciting from memory entire articles of this constitution, as well as ones from the constitution that established and nurtured the Republic of Cuba prior to Castro. Despite having strong words for the current leaders of the exiled community, Elpidio was a true Cuban nationalist hero, a believer that someday, somehow, a true democracy would find a hold on the island and flourish. But he knew that for this to happen sacrifices were needed by all Cubans, and a will for freedom — a backbone and courage. Elpidio despised the notion that foreign intervention was the only viable means of bringing change to Cuba, of defeating Castro. Instead, he held that freedom from foreign intervention, notably that of the United States, was what was needed in order to achieve the goals desired by Cubans. Elpidio rightly insisted that the Castro problem was a Cuban problem; therefore, the solution for that problem must come from Cubans themselves. He would paraphrase the founding fathers of the United States, using the principle of "by the people, for the people, and of the people," to underscore the argument that the solutions to Cuban problems would come by Cubans, and would be for Cubans, with the resultant peace of the Cuban people.

XIX

Conclusion

With the ongoing, seemingly endless war in Iraq, Cuba has been in the periphery of news reported in the US media. Most coverage has centered on the use of the US military facilities located at Guantánamo Bay. Other items have focused on the influence that Fidel Castro continues to command in Central and South America, as well as the Caribbean basin, where always he sees the slightest ray of opportunity. In 2002, there was a flurry of events within and surrounding Cuba that may have significant implications. Former president, Jimmy Carter traveled to Cuba, met with Castro and gave uncensored speeches. All of this was properly reported in the American media, even if newspapers buried it deep within their pages rather than risk attracting too much attention to the event. In 2006, Castro and Cuba continued to be in the news, with reported items ranging from Castro's stumble and fall at a political event, to photos with Elian Gonzalez (photo ops that seem to become more and more trite as they are repeatedly staged for the world to see) and stories such about Castro's relations with and Evo Morales, president of Bolivia, and Hugo Chávez, president of Venezuela. We should be beyond surprise when Castro meddles in other nations, in particular those that display the slightest inclination of a leftist leaning, a leaning well confirmed by both Chavez and Morales, without any doubt, through their actions and speeches. The recent appropriation of foreign-owned oil production facilities and fields in their countries brings a sense of "déjà vu all over again" for those among us who recall, or have studied, the blatant appropriations of oil refineries and other facilities in Cuba by Castro shortly after he took power.

Of all these events, it seems that the most significant to the Cuban people was Carter's visit to Cuba. While the uncensored speeches and unprecedented access to the Cuban populace are noteworthy, it is just as interesting to note other events that went either unnoticed or were just plain ignored by the US press. Prior to Carter's meeting with Castro,

Conclusion

Carter met with a few Cuban dissidents, learning firsthand about the "Projecto Varela," an ambitious project attempting to use the current communist constitution of Cuba to force a referendum upon Castro. The press focused on the fact that Carter was given wide access to the Cuban people, but failed to mention the content of his speeches, speeches that were significant not just for their direct critique of Castro and his regime, but also for their unprecedented, uncensored nature. For most Cubans on the island this was the first time that they had heard about the Varela movement, and with the wide dissemination of this information by Carter, Castro was forced to follow up with staged marches and events attempting to convince Cubans that there was no need for a referendum, that communist socialism is the only way to go. Then Castro mandated his puppet congress to incorporate new socialist measures permanently into the Cuban constitution, including an item that would prohibit any further questioning of his leadership or anyone calling for referendums in the future. Castro has reason to fear the Varela referendum, for a similar situation developed in Poland by an electrician named Lech Wałęsa, aided by Pope John Paul II and President Ronald Reagan, became instrumental in the fall of the communist rulers of Poland.

I am hopeful through this book, by facilitating stories of others, that a spark will be ignited, and the desire to be a part of the solution will inflame us all, that as we head together into the future, the courage and conviction of great men and women like Alberto Echenique will be assimilated into us to further strengthen our own courage and convictions.

Time and again leaders of the exiled Cuban community point out that Castro didn't "become" communist but instead embraced communism as the means to ensure that he would remain in power. Castro was willing to do whatever it would take to remain in control of Cuba, and his actions over nearly five decades leave no doubt as to his resolve to remain in power at all costs, including the deaths of untold numbers of his fellow Cubans.

The miserable Cuban economy has evolved after the collapse of the Soviet Union and with the end of subsidies from Moscow. The Cuba of 1950 was in many ways similar, yet very different from the Cuba of today. Even without Castro, the Cuban economy would have changed, as natural resources were exhausted, leading to changes of the mostly agrarian economy to other products or services. These market-controlled changes could have led to a Cuban economy that is sustainable, modern, and viable, rather than the system currently in place that is dependent on foreign injections of capital to keep it alive, although barely surviving, as more and more of Cuba's natural assets, as well as the soul of its people, are sacrificed for the entertainment and benefit of foreigners. The irony is that nearly five decades of Fidel Castro's rhetoric, of all his efforts to beat a nation into submission through a nationalistic, anti-American-imperialism agenda, have led not to a healthy, free and self-sufficient Cuba, but to an anemic, moribund Cuba heavily dependent on foreign aid. This aid has come directly from the United States in the past, not just through non-governmental agencies, but directly from the government, through the sale of items ranging from beef to apples.

The future is murky. It is difficult to see what the economy will be without Castro's disastrous policies. The impact of a successful transition to a tourist-based economy will be minimal at best. Cubans are a proud people; they will never be able to maintain the subservient attitude toward foreigners needed in a hospitality industry.

What about possible export products that have been proposed? There is the ever present Cuban sugar, but the United States produces more than enough, and subsidizes its own internal market through direct subsidies to growers. Other world markets appear minimal at best, as evident by the lack of interest in Cuban sugar following the collapse of the Soviet Union and the end of the Soviet's purchases. Cuba is now buying beef from United States, but could readily grow this industry with some influx of investment to a level that would satisfy internal demand, even if it does not become a net exporter. Citrus, notably oranges, have been proposed, but the United States produces more than enough, as do other countries, thereby creating the impression that this will be a difficult market to enter as an exporter. It certainly seems that it will be a challenge for any new government in a post-Castro Cuba to transition to a capitalist market economy, as viable products for the marketplace may be few and far between. But Cubans are a tenacious, resourceful people, with quite a few surprises left, so I wouldn't write them off the world market yet.

The research for this book has taken place over the course of several years, many hours hunched over a keyboard at my desk or on my laptop, in airports, on airplanes, in hotel rooms, as I traveled to and from Florida for interviews and family visits, and when I have traveled this great nation of ours in my employment. It has evolved from a simple college research paper to a work of love. Love for my friends and relatives, my fellow Cubans, here in the United States, abroad, and back home in Cuba. If you believe that I am trying to express an opinion through this work, you are correct. And in a nutshell, that opinion is that the embargo is a waste of time and effort. It is unjust toward millions of ordinary Cubans, in exile and at home, and after more than forty-seven years it is a failure, one that needs to go.

Many people were interviewed for this book, some more than once. Some of these interviews were very enlightening for me, and I hope I have shared that enlightenment with you. The majority of my sources were initially contacted through a simple questionnaire sent over the Internet, or made available at certain gatherings in Miami or elsewhere in South Florida. Some people took it upon themselves to further distribute the questionnaire to a greater group of exiled Cubans, and some provided me with direct referrals to individuals they considered well informed and knowledgeable about the American embargo, thus capable of providing an informed opinion. Sometimes the opinions were indeed informed, other times they were regurgitated propaganda that is heard daily on Miami talk radio shows, a hateful barrage that only serves to poison the air and the mind, while advancing the cause of a select few. Of all of the people who responded to the questionnaire or agreed to be interviewed, most provided snippets of how the embargo has affected their lives. Overall the common theme is one of hardship and sacrifice by individuals and families. Some of their relatives paid the ultimate price — death. Most Cubans are directly or indirectly affected by the embargo. Some are very cognizant of it; others either chose to ignore it, have become Americanized, or simply don't care anymore. But the fact remains that the embargo is a failed policy, and this policy affects the lives of many on a daily basis.

I found it interesting how exiled Cubans reacted to my questions about the embargo. There is definitely a trend among age groups, with most of the middle-age and older adults firmly in favor of the embargo, but that stance lessening, to a degree, the younger the people are. Of all the individuals with whom I communicated more than once, the great majority lessened their support of the embargo when it was privately discussed one-on-one. A surprising number, perhaps half, reversed their position when discussing it privately. This led me to believe that there is much more support among the exiled Cuban community to remove the embargo than what is generally accepted for this group. Although this was by no means a scientific poll, I do believe it is representative. Where does this herd mentality come from? It may be the result of decades of being told to "hang on a little longer, surely Castro will fall this year, all you have to do is vote for me," and other such lies that increase in direct proportion to how soon the next election will be held. Why does the exiled Cuban, a person known to be warm, generous and friendly, subscribe to a policy that affects not just fellow Cubans, but in many cases mothers, fathers, brothers and sisters left behind?

Cubans in a group tend to act like a pack, and quickly work each other into actions, much like a shark feeding frenzy. Cubans are such an energetic people, but individually most tend to be rational, thoughtful and agreeable. The majority of exiled Cubans support the embargo as a means to punish Castro and his regime. But half of these same individuals will admit that it is a failed policy once presented with an argument that this policy has not only failed to remove Castro from power, after more than four decades, but has created conditions such that the average Cuban lives in unimaginable poverty, while those in power live in relative comfort. These individuals can see how the removal of the embargo might increase interactions with Cubans on the island, which in turn would lead to greater desire and demand for personal and political freedom.

The ones who continue to puzzle me are those who maintain a virulent support for enforcing the embargo, come hell or high water, with no discussion, no exchange, only a "this is the way it must be, take or leave it mentality." It is easy to understand the position of some of these people, when viewed in the light of forty years of resentments, failed dreams and false expectations, coupled with a destroyed sense of hope. But for others, those who have had a good life as exiles, with successful careers and businesses, living a life of comfort, a life that would be like royalty to their counterparts back home in Cuba, those are the ones I fail to understand as they maintain an unwavering support for the embargo, an attitude of "if we have to cause Cubans' suffering in order to cause Castro to fall, then it must be so." We, as Cuban Americans and all Americans, would not accept that if forced upon us here in the United States. Where is our compassion?

Politicians tell us that we must not capitulate to Castro and his evil regime. These politicians paint a picture of Cuba as a country of human rights abuses, jails filled with political prisoners, and the lack of such basic rights as the freedom of speech and the freedom to assemble. These are but a few of many reasons given as to why we must not negotiate with Castro, why the embargo must remain in place. But if they are so willing to punish Castro and the political system in Cuba for these crimes and abuses, then what about China? What about North Korea? What about Saudi Arabia, the same country that produced the majority of the 9/11 hijackers, the country where women cannot vote and where trade in humans as slaves still occurs? That line from the original Bill Clinton presidential campaign comes to mind as a possible answer: "It's the economy, stupid." Our American leaders chose to ignore the abuses in these other countries because it serves them and our economy to do so. China is by large our greatest trading partner, never mind that some of those exports are made by prisoners in jail factories, work for which they are not compensated. We are told day after day that the United States is the only remaining superpower, a statement poured upon us by Washington relentlessly, a statement they apparently want us to take as a fact. As such, this "fact" will remain true until the day the Chinese sleeping dragon arises and decides to flex its economic muscles. What will happen then? Where will we get all of our goods if China decides to halt their exports into the United States? Wal-Mart's shelves will be empty quicker than any Category 4 hurricane threaten depletes plywood and bottle water socks in South Florida or the Gulf Coast. Most other stores, from mom-and-pops to big box, will be in the same quandary. (As a side note, whatever happened to Wal-Mart's "Made in America" campaign just a few years ago? Why does it seem that with the passing of Sam Walton the chain has morphed into an endless purveyor of cheap Chinese merchandise?)

The United States turns a blind eye and chooses to ignore the issues in these countries because it benefits the United States to do so. Never mind that these are the same issues it punishes Cuba for. But Cuba does not have the economic engine of China, nor the oil of Saudi Arabia, nor of Iraq, for that matter. Why did we invade Iraq, causing the death of tens of thousands, and the destruction of a nation's infrastructure? "Weapons of mass destruction" are what we were told by the Bush administration, the same weapons of mass destruction that the United Nations inspectors said did not exist. The same that Secretary of State Colin Powell said did not exist. Oil, plain and simple, was needed to continue lubricating the gears of the economic engine in the United States. It seems like the invasion and search was more an exercise of weapons of mass *distraction*. And Cuba? Cuba is kept like a pit bull chained to a tree in a backyard, and a short chain, at that, because it will not bow to our demands. Rather than attempt to train or teach the dog, we decide to shorten its chain even more, limit its food and water, as a means to teach it what we think it needs to know. And then we wonder why that dog not only just won't listen, but keeps trying to bite our hand.

Cuba does not offer much to the United States: not enough oil off her coasts, sugar prices kept low by governmental subsidies in the United States. Tourism is about all that is left, but then Cubans are not a subservient people; therefore tourism, if made accessible to Americans, would flourish for a brief period and then also falter. Besides, how many times are Ma and Pa from Indiana going to travel to Cuba? As long as Cuba does not offer any economic incentive for the United States, the American embargo will remain in place. That is unless an uncharacteristic politician comes along, one with vision, or at least empathy and compassion, one willing to remove the embargo, as the United States House of Representatives has voted to do time and again, only to see the measure stall in the Senate.

It is my premise that if we were to remove the American embargo, unilaterally with no conditions, democracy would return quickly to Cuba. What better way to get back at Fidel Castro than to invalidate all he has worked so hard to do and maintain. What could be better than to see Castro go from dictator to has been, living in fear while "retired" in some South American or African country, waiting for what happened to Charles Taylor or Slobodan Milosevic, or Saddam Hussein, forced to face tribunal for war crimes, or perhaps even the fate delivered to Nicaragua's General Somoza, his hiding days ended by the well-placed delivery of a rocket-propelled grenade, assassinated while enjoying his "retirement" in South America. While the demise of Fidel Castro will dominate the world news, Cuba, the *real* Cuba, will finally be able to return to the warm, life-giving embrace of democracy and freedom that we all so desire for her and that has eluded her grasp for too long.

Index

Index

Index

Index